Introduction to C++ for Engineers and Scientists

Delores M. Etter

Department of Electrical and Computer Engineering
University of Colorado, Boulder

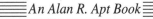
An Alan R. Apt Book

Prentice Hall, Upper Saddle River, NJ 07458

Library of Congress Cataloging–in–Publication Data

Etter, D. M.
    Introduction to C++ for engineers and scientists / Delores M.
Etter.
        p.   cm.
    Includes index.
    ISBN 0-13-254731-7
    1.   C++ (Computer program language)   1.   Title.
QA76.73.C153E85   1997
502'.85'5133--dc21

96-53667
CIP

Publisher: Alan Apt
Editor: Laura Steele
Project Manager: Jennifer Wenzel
Editorial/Production Supervisor: Sharyn Vitrano
Copy Editor: Brian Baker
Design Director: Heather Scott
Cover Designer: Rod Hernandez
Manufacturing Buyer: Donna Sullivan
Editorial Assistant: Shirley McGuire
Cover Photo: A DNA molecule model. Courtesy of FPG International.

In memory of my dearest Mother, Muerladene Janice Van Camp

© 1997 by Prentice-Hall, Inc.
Simon & Schuster / A Viacom Company
Upper Saddle River, New Jersey 07458

Printed in the United States of America

10   9   8   7   6   5   4   3   2

ISBN 0-13-254731-7

PRENTICE-HALL INTERNATIONAL (UK) LIMITED, *London*
PRENTICE-HALL OF AUSTRALIA PTY. LIMITED, *Sydney*
PRENTICE-HALL OF CANADA, INC., *Toronto*
PRENTICE-HALL HISPANOAMERICANA, S.A., *Mexico*
PRENTICE-HALL OF INDIA PRIVATE LIMITED, *New Delhi*
PRENTICE-HALL OF JAPAN, INC., *Tokyo*
SIMON & SCHUSTER ASIA PTE. LTD., *Singapore*
EDITORA PRENTICE-HALL DO BRASIL, LTDA., *Rio de Janeiro*

TRADEMARK INFORMATION

MATLAB is a registered trademark of
The MathWorks, Inc.

Preface

Engineers use computers to solve a variety of problems ranging from the evaluation of a simple function to solving a system of nonlinear equations. C++ has become the language of choice of many engineers and scientists because of its powerful commands and data structures and because it can easily be used for system-level operations. Since C++ is a language that a new engineer is likely to encounter in a job, it is a good choice for an introduction to computing for engineers. Therefore, this text was written to introduce engineering problem solving with the following objectives:

- to present a consistent **methodology for solving engineering problems,**
- to introduce the **fundamental capabilities of C++,** the language of choice of many practicing engineers and scientists, and
- to illustrate the problem-solving process with C++ through a variety of **engineering examples and applications.**

To accomplish these objectives, Chapter 1 presents a five-step process that is used in solving engineering problems, and Chapters 2–6 introduce the fundamental capabilities of C++ for solving engineering problems.

PREREQUISITES

No prior experience with the computer is assumed. The mathematical prerequisites are **college algebra and trigonometry.** Of course, the initial material can be covered much faster if the student has used other computer languages or software tools.

INTRODUCTION TO C++

Many schools are using their introductory engineering courses to acquaint students with a variety of computer tools and languages. As a result, this text was developed as a brief introduction to C++. An understanding of Chapters 1–3 is necessary to be able to write substantial C++ programs. Chapters 4–6 introduce additional topics, such as programmer-defined functions, one-dimensional arrays, and character data. In a typical introductory course, the material can be covered in six weeks.

PROBLEM-SOLVING METHODOLOGY

An important part of this text is its **emphasis on engineering and scientific problem solving.** Chapter 1 introduces a **five-step process for solving engineering problems** using the computer:

1. State the problem clearly.
2. Describe the input and output information.
3. Work a simple example by hand.
4. Develop an algorithm and convert it to a computer program.
5. Test the solution with a variety of data.

To reinforce the development of problem-solving skills, each of these five steps is clearly identified each time that a complete solution to an engineering problem is developed. In addition, **top-down design** and **stepwise refinement** are presented with the use of **decomposition outlines, pseudocode,** and **flowcharts**.

ENGINEERING AND SCIENTIFIC APPLICATIONS

Throughout the text, emphasis is placed on incorporating real-world engineering and scientific examples and problems. This emphasis is centered around a theme of **grand challenges,** which include:

- prediction of weather, climate, and global change
- computerized understanding of speech
- mapping of the human genome
- improvements in vehicle performance
- enhanced oil and gas recovery

Each chapter begins with a photograph and a discussion of some aspect of one of these grand challenges that provides a glimpse of some of the exciting and interesting areas in which engineers might work. The grand challenges also are referenced in many of the other examples and problems.

SOFTWARE ENGINEERING CONCEPTS

Engineers and scientists are expected to develop and implement **user-friendly** and **reusable** computer solutions. Learning software engineering techniques is crucial to developing these solutions successfully. **Readability** and **documentation,** therefore, are stressed in the development of the programs in this text. Additional topics that relate to software engineering are discussed throughout the text and include issues such as **the software life cycle, portability, maintenance, modularity, abstraction, reusability, and structured programming.**

EXERCISES AND PROBLEMS

Learning any new skill requires practice at a number of different levels of difficulty. Most sections of the text are immediately followed by a set of short-answer questions that relate to the material just presented. These **Practice! problems** are included so that students can determine whether they are ready to go on to the next section. Complete solutions to all the Practice! problems are presented at the end of the text.

Each chapter ends with a set of **end-of-chapter problems.** These are new problems that relate to a variety of engineering applications, and their level of difficulty ranges from very straightforward to more complex. Each problem requires that the student develop a complete C++ program or function. Engineering data sets are included for many of the problems to use in testing.

STUDENT AIDS

Margin notes are used to help the reader not only identify important concepts, but also locate specific topics easily. In addition, they are used to identify programming style guidelines and debugging information. Style guidelines show students how to write C++ programs that incorporate good software discipline; debugging sections help students recognize common errors so that they can avoid them. The programming style notes are indicated by the margin note *"Style,"* and the debugging notes are indicated with a **bug icon.** To make the book easier to use as a reference, each **Chapter Summary** contains a summary of the style notes and debugging notes, plus a list of the **Key Terms** from the chapter and a **C++ Statement Summary** of the new statements introduced in the chapter. Appendix A presents the **ASCII character codes.** In addition, the final two pages of the text contain information commonly used by students, including the operator precedence table, common C++ functions, common I/O operators and manipulators, and a C++ statement summary.

MATLAB AND VISUALIZATION

The visualization of the information related to a problem and its solution is a critical component in understanding and developing the intuition necessary to be a creative engineer. Therefore, we have included a number of plots of data throughout the text to illustrate the relationships of the information needed to solve specific problems. All the plots were generated using MATLAB, a powerful environment for numerical computations, data analysis, and visualization. For further information on MATLAB, we recommend two texts: *Engineering Problem Solving with MATLAB*, second edition, a complete presentation of the software, and *An Introduction to MATLAB for Engineers and Scientists*, a brief introduction. Both texts are written by Delores M. Etter, and are published by Prentice Hall Publishing Company.

INSTRUCTOR'S MANUAL

An **Instructor's Manual** is available that contains complete solutions to all the end-of-chapter problems. Also, transparency masters are included to assist in preparing lecture material.

ACKNOWLEDGMENTS

I first want to acknowledge the outstanding work of the publishing team at Prentice-Hall, including Alan Apt, Marcia Horton, Laura Steele, Sondra Chavez, Joel Berman, and Mike Sutton. Next, I want to thank Carla Williams (Fort Lewis College), Jeanine Ingber (University of New Mexico) and Jean Tan for their constructive and detailed comments on an early draft of this module. The text also has benefited significantly from the suggestions and comments of the reviewers of my earlier work, *Engineering Problem Solving with ANSI C: Fundamental Concepts* and *Introduction to ANSI C for Engineers and Scientists.* These reviewers included Arnold Robbins (Georgia Institute of Technology), Avelino Gonzalez (University of Central Florida), Thomas Cargill (private consultant), Jonathan Haines (Ball Aerospace Corp.), Thomas Walker (Virginia Polytechnic Institute and State University), Christopher Skelly (Insight Resource, Inc.), Betty Barr (University of Houston), John Cordero (University of Southern California), A. R. Marundarajan (California Polytechnic Institute Pomona), Lawrence Genalo (Iowa State University), Karen Davis (University of Cincinnati), Petros Gheresus (General Motors Institute), Leon Levine (University of California at Los Angeles), Harry Tyrer (University of Missouri–Columbia), Caleb Drake (University of Illinois at Chicago), John Miller (University of Michigan–Dearborn), Elden Heiden (New Mexico State University), Joe Hootman (University of North Dakota), and Nazeih Botros (Southern Illinois University).

I also want to express my gratitude to my husband, a mechanical/aerospace engineer, for his help in developing some of the engineering applications problems, and to my daughter, a veterinary student, for her help in developing some of the DNA-related material and problems. Finally, I want to recognize the important contributions of the students in my introductory engineering courses for their feedback on the explanations, the examples, and the problems.

Delores M. Etter
Department of Electrical/Computer Engineering
University of Colorado, Boulder

Contents

Introduction to C++ for Engineers and Scientists

10

Courtesy of Texas Instruments Incorporated.

GRAND CHALLENGE:
Weather Prediction

Weather satellites provide a great deal of information to meteorologists who attempt to predict the weather. Large volumes of historical weather data also can be analyzed and used to test models for predicting weather. In general, we do a reasonably good job of predicting overall weather patterns; however, local weather phenomena such as tornadoes, waterspouts, and microbursts are still very difficult to predict. Even predicting heavy rainfall or large hail from thunderstorms is often difficult. While Doppler radar is useful in locating regions within storms that could contain tornadoes or microbursts, the radar detects the events as they occur and thus gives little time for issuing appropriate warnings to populated areas or aircraft. The accurate and timely prediction of weather and associated phenomena is still an elusive goal.

An Introduction to Engineering Problem Solving

OBJECTIVES

Although most of this text is focused on introducing you to the C++ language, we begin by presenting a group of grand challenges—problems yet to be solved that will require technological breakthroughs in both engineering and science. One of these grand challenges is the prediction of weather, just mentioned in the chapter opening discussion. Since most solutions to engineering problems use computers, we next describe computer systems, including hardware and software. Solving engineering problems effectively with the computer also requires a design plan or procedure, so in this chapter we define a problem-solving methodology with five steps for describing a problem and then developing a solution.

1.1   Grand Challenges

Grand challenges

Engineers solve real-world problems using scientific principles from disciplines that include computer science, mathematics, physics, and chemistry. It is this variety of subjects, and the challenge of real problems, that makes engineering so interesting and so rewarding. In this section we present a group of **grand challenges**—fundamental problems in science and engineering with a potentially broad impact. The grand challenges were identified by the Office of Science and Technology Policy in Washington, DC, as part of a research and development strategy for high-performance computing. The following paragraphs briefly present some of these grand challenges and outline the types of benefits that will come with their solutions; additional discussions are presented at the beginning of the chapters. Just as the computer played an important part in the engineering achievements of the last 35 years, it will play an even greater role in solving problems related to the grand challenges.

Prediction of weather, climate, and global change

The **prediction of weather, climate, and global change** requires that we understand the coupled atmosphere and ocean biosphere system. This includes understanding CO_2 dynamics in the atmosphere and ocean, ozone depletion, and climatological changes due to releases of chemicals or energy into the atmosphere or ocean. Solar interactions play a part as well. For example, a major eruption from a solar storm near a "coronal hole" (a venting point for the solar wind) can eject vast amounts of hot gases from the sun's surface toward the earth's surface at speeds over a million miles per hour. This ejection of hot gases bombards the earth with X rays and can interfere with communication and cause fluctuations in power lines. Learning to predict weather, climate, and global changes involves collecting large amounts of data for study and developing new mathematical models that can represent the interdependency of many variables.

Computerized understanding of speech

The **computerized understanding of speech** could revolutionize our communication systems, but many problems are involved. Teaching a computer to understand words from a small vocabulary spoken by the same person is currently possible. However, developing systems that are speaker independent and that understand words from large vocabularies and from different languages is very difficult. Subtle changes in one's voice, such as those caused by a cold or stress, can affect the performance of speech recognition systems. Even assuming that the computer can recognize the words, it is not simple to determine their meaning. Many words are dependent on context and thus cannot be analyzed separately. Intonation, such as raising one's voice, can change a statement into a question. While there are still many difficult problems left to address in automatic speech recognition and understanding, exciting applications are everywhere. Imagine a telephone system that determines the languages being spoken and translates the speech signals so that each person hears the conversation in his or her native language.

Human Genome Project

The goal of the **Human Genome Project** is to locate, identify, and determine the function of each of the 50,000 to 100,000 genes contained in human deoxyribonucleic acid (DNA), which is the genetic material found in cells. The deciphering of the human genetic code will lead to many technical advances, including the ability to detect most, if not all, of the over 4,000 known human genetic diseases such as sickle-cell anemia and cystic fibrosis. However, deciphering the code is complicated by the nature of genetic information. Each gene is a double-helix strand composed of base pairs (adenine bonded with thymine or cytosine bonded with guanine) arranged in a steplike manner with phosphate groups along the side. These base pairs can occur in any order and represent the hereditary information in the gene. The number of base pairs in human DNA has been estimated to be around 3 billion. Because DNA directs the production of proteins for all metabolic needs, the proteins produced by a cell may provide a key to the sequence of base pairs in the DNA.

Improvements in vehicle performance

Substantial **improvements in vehicle performance** require more complex physical modeling in the areas of fluid dynamic behavior for three-dimensional flow fields and flow inside engine turbomachinery and ducts. Turbulence in fluid flows affects the stability and control, thermal characteristics, and fuel performance of aerospace vehicles, and modeling the flow is necessary for the analysis of new configurations. The analysis of the aeroelastic behavior of vehicles influences new designs as well. The efficiency of combustion systems is also related because attaining significant improvements in combustion efficiency requires understanding the relationships between the flows of the various substances and the chemistry that causes the substances to react. One way vehicle performance is being addressed is through the use of onboard computers and microprocessors. Transportation systems are currently being studied in which cars have computers with small video screens mounted on the dash. The driver enters the location of the destination, and the video screen shows the street names and a path to get from the current location to the desired location. A communication network keeps the car's computer aware of any traffic jams so that it can automatically reroute the car if necessary. Other transportation research addresses totally automated driving, with computers and networks handling all the control and interchange of information.

Enhanced oil and gas recovery

Enhanced oil and gas recovery will allow us to locate the estimated 300 billion barrels of oil reserves in the United States. Current methods for identifying structures likely to contain oil and gas use seismic techniques that can evaluate structures down to 20,000 feet below the surface. These techniques use a group of sensors (called a sensor array) that is located near the area to be tested. A ground shock signal, sent into the earth, is reflected by the boundaries between the different geological layers and is then received by the sensors. By means of sophisticated signal processing, the boundary layers can be mapped, and some estimate can be made as to the materials in the various layers, such as sandstone, shale, and water. The ground shock signals can be generated in several ways: A hole can be drilled and an explosive charge exploded in it; a ground shock can be generated by an explosive charge on the surface; or a special truck that uses a hydraulic hammer can be used to pound the earth several times per second. Continued research is needed to improve the resolution of the information that is received and to find methods of production and recovery that are economical and ecologically sound.

These grand challenges are only a few of the many interesting problems waiting to be solved by engineers and scientists. The solutions to problems of this magnitude will be the result of organized approaches that combine ideas and technologies. The use of computers and engineering problem-solving techniques will be a key element in the solution process.

1.2 Computing Systems

Program

Before we present the language C++, a brief discussion on computing is useful, especially for those who have not had prior experience with computers. A **computer** is a machine that is designed to perform operations that are specified with a set of instructions called a **program**. Computer **hardware** consists of equipment such as the computer keyboard, the mouse, the terminal, the hard disk, and the printer. Computer **software** comprises the programs that describe the steps we want the computer to perform.

COMPUTER HARDWARE

*Arithmetic
logic unit*

All computers have a common internal organization, as shown in Figure 1.1. The **control unit** is the part of the computer that directs the interaction of all the other parts. It accepts input values (from a device such as a keyboard) and stores them in the **memory**. It also interprets the instructions in a computer program. If we want to add two values, the control unit will retrieve the values from memory and send them to the **arithmetic logic unit**, or **ALU**. The ALU performs the addition, and the control unit then stores the result in memory. The control unit and the ALU use internal memory composed of read-only memory (ROM) and random-access memory (RAM) in their processing; most data are stored in external memory or secondary memory using hard disk drives or floppy disk drives that are attached to the processor. The control unit and ALU together are called the **central processing unit**, or **CPU**. A **microprocessor** is a CPU that is contained in a single integrated circuit chip which contains millions of components in an area smaller than a postage stamp.

We usually instruct the computer to print the values that it has computed on the screen of the terminal or on paper using a printer. Dot matrix printers use a matrix (or grid) of pins to produce the shape of a character on paper, while a

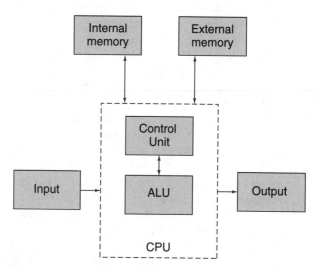

Figure 1.1 *Internal organization of a computer.*

laser printer uses a light beam to transfer images to paper. The computer can also write information to diskettes, which store the information magnetically. A printed copy of information is called a **hard copy**, and a magnetic copy of information is called an **electronic copy** or a soft copy.

PCs

Computers come in all sizes, shapes, and forms. (See the photos on the next page.) Personal computers (**PCs**) are small, inexpensive computers that are commonly used in offices, homes, and laboratories. PCs are also referred to as microcomputers, and their design is built around a microprocessor chip, such as the Intel 486 and Pentium microprocessors, which can process millions of instructions per second (mips). Minicomputers are more powerful than microcomputers and typically support more than one user at a time through time-sharing. Mainframes are even more powerful computers that are often used in businesses and research laboratories. A **workstation** is a minicomputer or mainframe computer that is small enough to fit on a desktop. **Supercomputers** are the fastest of all computers and can process billions of instructions per second (bips). As a result, they are capable of solving very complex problems that cannot be feasibly solved on other computers. Mainframes and supercomputers require special facilities and a specialized staff to run and maintain the computer systems.

Networks

The type of computer needed to solve a particular problem depends on the requirements of the problem. If the computer is part of a home security system, a microprocessor is sufficient; if the computer is running a flight simulator, a mainframe is probably needed. Computer **networks** allow computers to communicate with each other so that they can share resources and information. For example, ethernet is a commonly used local area network (LAN).

COMPUTER SOFTWARE

Computer software contains the instructions or commands that we want the computer to perform. Several important categories of software are operating systems, software tools, and language compilers. Figure 1.2 illustrates the interaction between each of these categories of software and the computer hardware.

Operating system

Operating systems. As an interface between you (the user) and the computer hardware, the **operating system** provides a convenient and efficient environment in which you can select and execute the software on your system. Typically, the operating system comes with the computer hardware when it is purchased.

Operating systems contain a group of programs called **utilities** that allow you to perform functions such as printing files, copying files from one diskette to another, and listing the files that you have saved on a diskette. While these utilities are common to most operating systems, the commands themselves vary from computer to computer. For example, to list your files using DOS ("Disk Operating System," used mainly with PCs), the command is dir; to list your files with UNIX (a powerful operating system frequently used with workstations), use the command ls. Some operating systems have a user-friendly **graphical user interface** (GUI); examples of such systems are the Macintosh environment and the Windows environment.

Graphical user interface

Because C++ programs can be run on many different platforms or hardware systems, and because a specific computer can use different operating systems, it

Courtesy of Johnson Space Center.

Courtesy of The Image Works.

Courtesy of Apple Computer Inc.

Courtesy of The Image Works.

Courtesy of CRAY Research.

Courtesy of IBM.

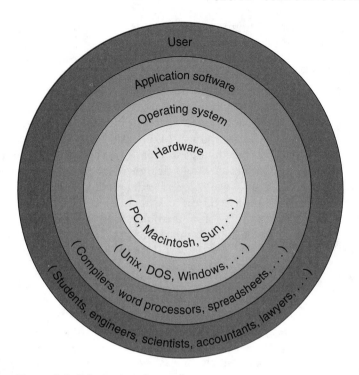

Figure 1.2 *Software interface to the computer.*

is not feasible to discuss the wide variety of operating systems that you might use while taking this course. We assume that your professor will provide the specific operating system information that you need to know to use the computers available at your university; this information is also contained in the operating system manuals.

Word processors

Software Tools. Software tools are programs that have been written to perform common operations. For example, **word processors** such as Microsoft Word and Word Perfect are programs that have been written to help you enter and format text. Word processors allow you to move sentences and paragraphs, and often have capabilities that permit you to enter mathematical equations and to check your spelling and grammar. Word processors are also used to enter computer programs and store them in files. Very sophisticated word processors allow you to produce well-designed pages that combine elaborate charts and graphics with text and headlines; these word processors use a technology called **desktop publishing**, which combines a very powerful word processor with a high-quality printer to produce professional-looking documents.

Spreadsheet

Spreadsheet programs are software tools that allow you to work easily with data that can be displayed in a grid of rows and columns. Spreadsheets were initially used for financial and accounting applications, but today they help solve many science and engineering problems. Most spreadsheet packages include plotting capabilities, so they can be especially useful in analyzing and displaying information. Lotus 1-2-3, Quattro Pro, and Excel are popular spreadsheet packages.

Database management

Another popular group of software tools are **database management** programs, such as dBase IV and Paradox. These programs allow you to store a large amount of data and then easily retrieve pieces of the data and format the information into reports. Databases are used by large organizations such as banks, hospitals, hotels, and airlines. Scientists and engineers use scientific databases to analyze large amounts of data. Meteorological data are one kind of scientific data that is stored in large databases for subsequent analysis.

Computer-aided design

Computer-aided design (CAD) packages such as AutoCAD, AutoSketch, and CADKEY allow you to define objects and then manipulate them graphically. For example, you can define an object and then view it from different angles or observe a rotation of the object from one position to another.

Mathematical computation

Some software packages, such as MATLAB, Mathematica, MATHCAD, and Maple, are very powerful **mathematical computation** tools. Not only do these tools incorporate mathematical commands, but they also provide extensive capabilities for generating graphs. This combination of computational power and visualization makes these packages particularly useful tools for engineers.

If an engineering problem can be solved using an existing software tool, it is usually more efficient to use the tool than to write a program in a computer language to solve the problem. However, many problems cannot be solved using current software tools, or a software tool may not be available on the computer system that must be used for solving the problem; thus, we also need to know how to write programs in various computer languages. In fact, the distinction between a software tool and a computer language is becoming less clear as some of the more powerful tools such as MATLAB and Mathematica include their own programming languages in addition to specialized operations. An understanding of computer languages and related problem solving also is helpful in using programmable calculators.

Computer Languages. Computer languages can be described in terms of levels.

Machine language

Machine language is the lowest level, most primitive language and is tied closely to the design of the computer hardware. Since computer designs are based on two-state technology (such as open or closed circuits, on or off switches, and positive or negative charges), machine language is written using two symbols, which are usually represented by the binary digits 0 and 1 (also called **bits**). Therefore, machine language is a **binary** language, with instructions that are written as sequences of 0's and 1's called binary strings. Because of the close tie between machine language and the design of the computer hardware, the machine language for a Sun computer is different from the machine language for a Silicon Graphics computer.

Assembly language

An **assembly language** is also unique to a specific computer design, but its instructions are written in English-like statements instead of binary. Assembly languages usually do not have very many statements; thus, writing programs in assembly language can be tedious. In addition, to use an assembly language, you must possess information that relates to the specific computer hardware. For example, **real-time programs** (programs that respond quickly to changing input, as in autopilot systems in airplanes) are often written directly in assembly language to take advantage of the specific computer hardware in order to increase the speed of their response.

High-level languages are computer languages that have English-like commands and instructions; they include languages such as C++, C, Fortran, Ada, Pascal, COBOL, and BASIC. Writing programs in a high-level language is certainly easier than writing programs in machine language or in assembly language. However, a high-level language contains a large number of commands and an extensive set of **syntax** (or grammar) rules for using the commands. To illustrate the syntax and punctuation required by both software tools and high-level languages, we compute the area of a circle with a specified diameter in Table 1.1 using several different languages and tools. Notice both the similarities and the differences in the statements that execute this simple computation. High-level language programs are usually portable, so they can be run on many different types of computers. Although we include C++ and C as high-level languages, many people like to describe them as midlevel languages because they allow access to low-level routines.

Languages are also defined in terms of **generations**. The first generation of computer languages was machine language, the second generation was assembly language, and the third generation, which is prevalent today, is high-level language. Fourth-generation languages, also referred to as **4GLs**, have not been developed yet and are described only in terms of their characteristics and programmer productivity. The fifth generation of languages is called natural language. To program in a fifth-generation language, one would use the syntax of natural speech. Clearly, the implementation of a natural language as a computer language would require the achievement of one of the grand challenges—the computerized understanding of speech.

Fortran (FORmula TRANslation) was developed in the mid-1950s for solving engineering and scientific problems. New standards updated the language over the years, and the current standard, Fortran 90, contains strong numerical computation capabilities, along with many of the new features and structures in languages such as C. **COBOL** (COmmon Business-Oriented Language) was developed in the late 1950s to solve business problems. **Basic** (Beginner's All-purpose Symbolic Instruction Code) was developed in the mid-1960s and was (and still is) used as an educational tool. It is often included with the system software for a PC. **Pascal** was developed in the early 1970s and has been widely used in computer science programs to introduce students to computing. **Ada** was developed at the initiative of the U.S.

High-level
languages

TABLE 1.1 Comparison of Software Statements

Software	Sample Statement
C++	`area = 3.141593*(diameter/2)*(diameter/2);`
C	`area = 3.141593*(diameter/2)*(diameter/2);`
MATLAB	`area = pi*((diameter/2)^2);`
Fortran	`area = 3.141593*(diameter/2.0)**2`
Ada	`area := 3.141593*(diameter/2)**2;`
Pascal	`area := 3.141593*(diameter/2)*(diameter/2)`
BASIC	`let a = 3.141593*(d/2)*(d/2)`
COBOL	`compute area = 3.141593*(diameter/2)*(diameter/2).`

Department of Defense with the purpose of developing a high-level language appropriate to embedded computer systems, typically implemented using microprocessors. The final design of the language was accepted in 1979. Ada was named in honor of Ada Lovelace, who developed instructions for doing computations on an analytical machine in the early 1800s. **C** is a general-purpose language that evolved from two languages, BCPL and B, which were developed at Bell Laboratories in the late 1960s. In 1972, Dennis Ritchie developed and implemented the first C compiler on a DEC PDP-11 computer at AT&T Bell Laboratories. The language became very popular for system development because it was hardware independent. As a result of its popularity in both industry and academia, a committee of the American National Standards Institute (ANSI) was created in 1983 to provide a machine-independent, unambiguous definition of C. In 1989, the **ANSI C** standard was approved. **C++** is an evolution of the language C that was developed at AT&T Bell Laboratories in the early 1980s by Bjarne Stroustrup. The extensions to C provided additional operators and functions that support creating and using data abstractions, as well as object-oriented design and programming.

C++

C++ has become the language of choice of many software professionals, engineers, and scientists not only because it has powerful commands and data structures, but also because it can easily be used for system-level operations. Since C++ is one of the languages that a new engineer is most likely to encounter in a job, it is a good choice for an introduction to computing for engineers. However, it is more important to establish a good foundation in an introductory course in computing than it is to cover all the features of the language. Therefore, only the most important features of C++ for solving engineering problems have been selected for this text. We thus provide an introduction to the fundamental concepts of C++ and do not attempt to cover all elements of the language.

Executing a Computer Program. A program written in a high-level language such as C++ must be translated into machine language before the instructions can be executed by the computer. A special program called a **compiler** is used to perform this translation. Thus, in order to be able to write and execute C++ programs on a computer, the computer's software must include a C++ compiler. C++ compilers are available for a wide range of computer hardware and operating system platforms, from supercomputers to personal computers.

Compiler

During the translation process, if any errors (often called **bugs**) are detected by the compiler, corresponding error messages are printed. We correct our program statements and then compile the program again. The errors identified during compilation are called **compile errors** or compile-time errors. For example, if we want to divide the value stored in a variable called sum by 3, the correct expression in C++ is sum/3; if we incorrectly write the expression using the backslash (sum\3), we will get a compile error. The process of compiling, correcting statements (or **debugging**), and recompiling often must be repeated several times before a program compiles without errors. When there are no compile errors, the compiler generates a program in machine language that performs the steps specified by the original C++ program. The latter is referred to as the **source program**, and the machine language version is called the **object program**. Thus, the source program

Debugging

and the object program describe the same steps, but the source program is specified in a high-level language and the object program is specified in machine language.

Execution

Once the program has compiled correctly, additional steps are necessary to prepare the object program for **execution**. This preparation involves **linking** other machine language statements to the object program and then **loading** the program into memory. After this linking/loading, the program is executed by the computer. New errors called execution errors, run-time errors, or **logic errors** may be identified at this stage; they are also called program bugs. Execution errors often cause the program to terminate. For example, the program may attempt to perform a division by zero, which generates an execution error. Some execution errors do not stop the program from executing, but cause incorrect results to be computed. These types of errors are often the result of mistakes on the part of the programmer, or they may be caused by errors in the data used by the program. When execution errors occur due to errors in the source program, we must correct the errors and recompile the program. Even when a program appears to execute properly, we must check the answers carefully to make sure that they are correct. The computer will perform the steps precisely as we specify, and if we specify the wrong steps, the computer will execute these wrong (but syntactically valid) steps and present us with an answer that is incorrect.

The processes of compilation, linking/loading, and execution are outlined in Figure 1.3. The process of converting an assembly language program to binary is performed by an **assembler** program, and the corresponding processes are called assembly, linking/ loading, and execution.

A C++ compiler often has additional capabilities that provide a user-friendly environment for implementing and testing C++ programs. For example, some C++ environments contain text processors so that program files can be generated, compiled, and executed in the same software package, as opposed to using a separate word processor that requires the use of operating system commands to transfer information back and forth between the word processor and the compiler. Many C++ programming environments include **debugger** programs, which are useful in identifying errors in a source program. Debugger programs allow us to see values stored in variables at different points in a program and to step through the program line by line.

As we present new statements in C++, we will point out common errors associated with the statements, as well as useful techniques for locating these

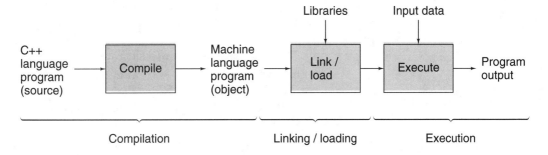

Figure 1.3 *Program compilation/linking/execution.*

errors. The **debugging aids** will be identified with a bug icon in the margin and will be summarized at the end of each chapter.

Software Life Cycle. In 1955, the cost of a typical computer solution was estimated to be 15% for the software development and 85% for the associated computer hardware. Over the years, the cost of the hardware has gone down dramatically, while the cost of the software has increased. In 1985 it was estimated that the numbers had essentially switched, with 85% of the cost going for software and 15% for hardware. With the majority of the cost of a computer solution now residing in software development, a great deal of attention has been given to understanding the steps involved in the completion of a software project, collectively called the **software life cycle**. These steps typically include the project definition, the detailed specification, coding and modular testing, integrated testing, and maintenance. Research indicates that the effort involved in each of these steps is as shown in Table 1.2. From these figures, it is clear that **software maintenance** is a significant part of the cost of a software system. This maintenance includes enhancing the software, fixing errors identified as the software is used, and adapting the software to work with new hardware and software. The ease of providing maintenance is directly related to the original definition of the problem and specification of the solution, because these steps lay the foundation for the rest of the project. The problem-solving process that we present in the next section emphasizes the need to define the problem and specify the solution carefully before beginning to code or test the resulting system.

Software maintenance

One of the techniques that has been successful in reducing both the time and cost of software development is the creation and use of **software prototypes**. Instead of waiting until the entire software system is developed before letting users work with it, a prototype of the system is created early in the process. This prototype does not have all the functionality required of the final software, but it does allow users to test it early in the life cycle and make modifications to the specifications based on the test results. Making changes earlier in the life cycle is both cost and time effective.

Software prototypes

As an engineer, you will very likely need to modify existing software. The modifications will be much simpler if the existing software is well structured and readable and if the documentation that accompanies the software is up to date and clearly written. For these reasons, we stress developing good habits that make programs more readable and self-documenting. As new C++ statements are

TABLE 1.2 Software Life Cycle Phases	
Life Cycle	Percent of Effort
Definition	3%
Specification	15%
Coding and Modular Testing	14%
Integrated Testing	8%
Maintenance	60%

presented and new techniques demonstrated in this text, we include guidelines for writing well-structured and readable code. These **style guidelines** are indicated with notes in the margin and are summarized at the end of each chapter.

1.3   An Engineering Problem-Solving Methodology

Problem solving is a key part of not only engineering courses, but also courses in computer science, mathematics, physics, and chemistry. Therefore, it is important to have a consistent approach to solving problems. It is also helpful if the approach is general enough to work for all these different areas, so that we do not have to learn a technique for mathematics problems, a different technique for physics problems, and so on. The **problem-solving methodology** that we present works for engineering problems and can be tailored to solve problems in other areas as well; it assumes, however, that we will make use of the computer to help solve the problem.

Problem-solving methodology

The process or methodology for problem solving that we will use throughout this text has **five steps:**

1.   State the problem clearly.
2.   Describe the input and output information.
3.   Work the problem by hand (or with a calculator) for a simple set of data.
4.   Develop a solution and convert it to a computer program.
5.   Test the solution with a variety of data.

Let us discuss each of these steps, using as an example the computation of the distance between two points in a plane.

1.   PROBLEM STATEMENT

The first step is to state the problem clearly. It is extremely important to give a clear, concise statement of the problem to avoid misunderstandings. For this example, we state the problem as follows:

Compute the straight-line distance between two points in a plane.

2.   INPUT/OUTPUT DESCRIPTION

The second step is to describe carefully the information that is given to solve the problem and then identify the values to be computed. This information represents the input and the output for the problem and can be called input/output or I/O. For many problems, a diagram that shows the input and output is useful. At this point the program is an abstraction, because we are not yet defining the steps to determine the output; instead, we are only specifying

I/O diagram

the information that is necessary to compute the output. The **I/O diagram** for this example is as follows:

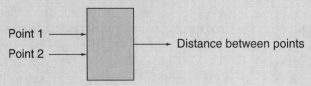

3.   HAND EXAMPLE

The third step is to work the problem by hand or with a calculator, using a simple set of data. This is a very important step and should not be skipped even for simple problems. It is the step in which you work out the details of the solution to the problem. If you cannot take a simple set of numbers and compute the output (either by hand or with a calculator), then you are not ready to move on to the next step; you should reread the problem and perhaps consult reference material. The solution by hand for this specific example is as follows:

Let the points p_1 and p_2 have the following coordinates (in centimeters):

$$p_1 = (1,5); \qquad p_2 = (4,7)$$

We want to compute the distance between the two points, which is the hypotenuse of a right triangle, as shown in the sketch in Figure 1.4. Using the Pythagorean theorem, we can compute the distance with the following equation:

$$\begin{aligned}
\text{distance} &= \sqrt{(\text{side}_1)^2 + (\text{side}_1)^2} \\
&= \sqrt{(4-1)^2 + (7-5)^2} \\
&= \sqrt{13} \\
&= 3.605551 \text{ cm}
\end{aligned}$$

4.   ALGORITHM DEVELOPMENT

Algorithm

Once you can work the problem for a simple set of data, you will be ready to develop an **algorithm,** or a step-by-step outline of the solution to the problem. For simple problems such as this one, the algorithm can be listed as operations that are performed one after another. The following outline decomposes our problem into simpler steps:

Decomposition Outline:
1. *Give values to the two points.*
2. *Compute the lengths of the two sides of the right triangle generated by the two points.*

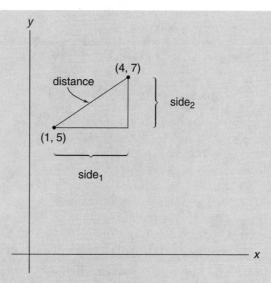

Figure 1.4 *Straight-line distance between two points.*

3. *Compute the distance between the two points, which is equal to the length of the hypotenuse of the triangle.*
4. *Print the distance between the two points.*

This **decomposition outline** is converted to C++ commands so that we can use the computer to perform the computations. From the following solution, you can see that the commands are very similar to the steps used in the hand example. The details of these commands are explained in Chapter 2.

```
//-----------------------------------------------------------
//  Program chapter 1_1
//
//  This program computes the
//  distance between two points.

#include <iostream.h>
#include <stdlib.h>
#include <math.h>

int main()
{
    //  Define and initialize variables.
    double x1=1, y1=5, x2=4, y2=7,
           side_1, side_2, distance;

    //  Compute sides of a right triangle.
    side_1 = x2 - x1;
    side_2 = y2 - y1;
    distance = sqrt(side_1*side_1 + side_2*side_2);
```

```
        //  Print distance.
        cout << "The distance between the two points is "
            << distance << " cm." << endl;

        //  Exit program.
        return EXIT_SUCCESS;
    }
    //----------------------------------------------------------
```

5.   TESTING

The final step in our problem-solving process is testing the solution. We should first test it with the data from the hand example, since we have already computed this solution. When the C++ statements in the preceding program are executed, the computer displays the following output:

`The distance between the two points is 3.605551 cm.`

The value for the distance stated in the output matches the value that we calculated by hand.

If the C++ solution does not match the hand solution, then we should review both solutions to find the error. Once the solution works for the hand example, we should test it with additional sets of (valid and invalid) data to be sure that it works for the valid sets.

The steps demonstrated in this example are used in developing the programs in the "Problem Solving Applied" sections in the chapters that follow.

CHAPTER SUMMARY

A set of grand challenges was presented to illustrate some of the exciting and difficult problems that currently face engineers and scientists. Because the solutions to most engineering problems, including the grand challenges, will be by computer, we also presented a summary of the components of a computer system, from computer hardware to computer software. We introduced a five-step problem-solving methodology that we will use to develop a computer solution to a problem. The five steps are as follows:

1.   State the problem clearly.
2.   Describe the input and output information.
3.   Work the problem by hand (or with a calculator) for a simple set of data.

4. Develop an algorithm and convert it to a computer program.

5. Test the solution with a variety of data.

This process will be used throughout the text as we develop solutions to problems.

KEY TERMS

algorithm	logic error
ANSI C	machine language
arithmetic logic unit (ALU)	mathematical tool
assembler	memory
assembly language	microprocessor
binary	network
bug	object program
C++	operating system
central processing unit (CPU)	personal computer (PC)
compiler	problem-solving methodology
compile error	processor
computer	program
computer-aided design	real-time program
database management	software
debug	software life cycle
debugger	software maintenance
decomposition outline	software prototype
desktop publishing	software tool
electronic copy	source program
execution	spreadsheet
grand challenges	supercomputer
hardware	syntax
high-level language	utility
I/O diagram	word processor
linking/loading	workstation

2

Courtesy of National Aeronautics and Space Administration.

GRAND CHALLENGE:
Vehicle Performance

Wind tunnels are test chambers built to generate precise wind speeds. Accurate scale models of new aircraft can be mounted on force-measuring supports in the test chamber, and measurements of the forces on the models can then be made at many different wind speeds and angles. Some wind tunnels can operate at hypersonic velocities, generating wind speeds of thousands of miles per hour. The size of wind tunnel test sections vary from a few inches across to sizes large enough to accommodate a jet fighter. At the completion of a wind tunnel test series, many sets of data have been collected that can be used to determine the lift, drag, and other aerodynamic performance characteristics of a new aircraft at its various operating speeds and positions.

Simple C++ Programs

OBJECTIVES

In this chapter, we outline the structure of a simple C++ program that defines variables, performs computations, and prints the results thereof. We then present the syntax and the semantics for the C++ statements that define and initialize constants and variables, that compute new values using simple arithmetic operations, that read user-supplied information from the keyboard during the execution of a program, and that print information on the screen. Additional functions are presented for most of the numerical computations commonly used to solve engineering problems. With these C++ statements and functions, we have the capability to write complete programs.

2.1   Program Structure

General
structure

In this section, we analyze the structure of a specific C++ program, and then we present the **general structure** of a C++ program. The following program, introduced in Chapter 1, computes and prints the distance between two points:

```
//-----------------------------------------------------------
//   Program chapter 1_1
//
//   This program computes the
//   distance between two points.

#include <iostream.h>
#include <stdlib.h>
#include <math.h>

int main()
{
   //  Define and initialize variables.
   double x1=1, y1=5, x2=4, y2=7,
          side_1, side_2, distance;

   //  Compute sides of a right triangle.
   side_1 = x2 - x1;
   side_2 = y2 - y1;
   distance = sqrt(side_1*side_1 + side_2*side_2);

   //  Print distance.
   cout << "The distance between the two points is "
        << distance << " cm." << endl;

   //  Exit program.
   return EXIT_SUCCESS;
}
//-----------------------------------------------------------
```

We now briefly discuss the statements in the program; each is discussed in detail later in the chapter.

Comments

The first five lines of the program contain **comments** that give the program a name **(chapter1_1)** and define its purpose:

```
//-----------------------------------------------------------
//   Program chapter 1_1
//
//   This program computes the
//   distance between two points.
```

There are two methods for inserting comments in a C++ program: A comment can begin with the characters //, or a comment can begin with the characters /* and end with the characters */. A comment can be on a line by itself, or it can be on the same line with a command. If a comment precedes a command on the

Style

same line, then it must be specified with the characters /* and */ because all information following // on a line is assumed to be a comment. *While comments are optional, good style requires that they be used throughout a program to improve its readability and to document the computations in the program.*

In the programs in the text, we use initial comments to give a name to the program and to describe the general purpose of the program; additional, explanatory comments are also included throughout the program. C++ allows comments and statements to begin anywhere on a line; we begin the initial comments of a program in the first column. We also use comment lines containing dashes as the first and last lines of a program to make it easy to identify the beginning and ending of the program.

Preprocessor directives

Preprocessor directives give instructions to the compiler that are performed before the program is compiled. The most common directive inserts additional statements in the program; it contains the characters **#include** followed by the name of the file containing the additional statements. The program to compute the distance between two points contains the following three preprocessor directives:

```
#include <iostream.h>
#include <stdlib.h>
#include <math.h>
```

Standard C++ library

These three directives specify that the statements in the files **iostream.h**, **stdlib.h**, and **math.h** should be inserted in place of the directives before the program is compiled. The **angle brackets** < and > around the file names indicate that the files are included in the **Standard C++ library,** which is contained in the files that accompany a C++ compiler. Note that there is no space between the angle brackets and the file name in an **include** directive.

The **iostream.h** file contains information related to the output statement used in this program, the **stdlib.h** file contains a constant we use in exiting the program, and the **math.h** file contains information related to the function used in the program to compute the square root of a value. The **h** extension on these file names specifies that the files are header files; more information on header files is included later in this chapter and in Chapter 4. Preprocessor directives are generally included after the initial comments describing the program's purpose. Preprocessor directives do not end with a semicolon.

Every C++ program contains a function named **main**. In Chapter 4 we will see that a function can be written to return a value, or it can be written as a **void** function that does not return a value. In our sample program, the word **main** is preceded by **int** to indicate that the **main** function returns an integer that can be used by the operating system. The body of the function is enclosed by braces, { and }. In order to identify the body of the function easily, we choose to place these braces on lines by themselves. Thus, the two lines following the preprocessor directives specify the beginning of the **main** function:

```
int main()
{
```

The **main** function contains two types of statements: statements that define memory locations which will be used in the program and statements that specify actions to be taken. Memory locations must be defined before they are used by other statements; **initial values** can also be specified at the time memory locations are defined.

A comment precedes the definition statement in the program:

```
//  Define and initialize variables.
double x1=1, y1=5, x2=4, y2=7,
       side_1, side_2, distance;
```

This statement specifies that the program will use seven variables, named **x1**, **y1**, **x2**, **y2**, **side_1**, **side_2**, and **distance**. The term **double** indicates that the variables will store double-precision floating-point values, such as 12.5 and -0.0005. In addition, the statement specifies that **x1** should be initialized to the value 1, **y1** should be initialized to the value 5, **x2** should be initialized to the value 4, and **y2** should be initialized to the value 7. The initial values of **side_1**, **side_2**, and **distance** are not specified and should not be assumed to be initialized to zero.

Style

Because the definition was too long for one line, we split it over two lines; the indenting of the second line is for readability.

The **statements** that specify the operations to be performed in the program are the following:

```
//  Compute sides of a right triangle.
side_1 = x2 - x1;
side_2 = y2 - y1;
distance = sqrt(side_1*side_1 + side_2*side_2);

//  Print distance.
cout << "The distance between the two points is "
     << distance << " cm." << endl;
```

These statements compute the lengths of the two sides of the right triangle formed by the two points (see Figure 1.4) and then compute the length of the hypotenuse of the right triangle. The details of the syntax of the statements are discussed later in the chapter. After the distance is computed, it is printed with the **cout** statement, which sends the specified output to the terminal screen. The **insertion operator** << separates different parts of the output. In this example, the output line contains the characters **The distance between the two points is**, followed by the value of the variable **distance**; then the characters **cm.** are inserted. The **endl** reference causes the output line to be displayed on the screen. Note that the definitions and statements are all required to end with a semicolon.

To exit the program, we use a **return** statement. The integer constant **EXIT_SUCCESS**, defined in the **stdlib.h** file, is returned to the operating system to indicate a successful exit from the program.

```
//  Exit program.
return EXIT_SUCCESS;
```

The use of a **return** statement at the end of the **main** function is optional in C++; we use it for documentation purposes.

The body of the **main** function ends with the right brace, and another comment line delineates the end of the function.

```
   }
   //------------------------------------------------------------
```

Style

Note that we have included blank lines (also called **white space**) in the program to separate the different components. *These blank lines make a program more readable and easier to modify.* The statements within the **main** function were indented three columns in order to show the structure of the program. This spacing provides a consistent style and makes our programs easier to read.

Now that we have closely examined the C++ program from Chapter 1, we can compare its structure with the typical form of a simple C++ program:

```
introductory comments
preprocessing directives
int main()
{
      statements;
}
```

This structure is evident in the programs developed in this chapter and in the chapters that follow.

2.2   Constants and Variables

Constants and variables represent values that we use in our programs. **Constants** are specific values such as 2, 3.1416, or −1.5 that we include in the C++ statements, while **variables** are memory locations that are assigned a name or identifier. The **identifier** is used to reference the value stored in the memory location. A useful analogy for a memory location and its corresponding identifier is a mailbox that is associated with the name of an individual; the memory location (or mailbox) then contains a value. The following diagram shows the variables, their identifiers, and their initial values after the definition statement from Program **chapter1_1** is executed:

Identifier

```
double x1=1, y1=5, x2=4, y2=7,
       side_1, side_2, distance;
```

x1	1	y1	5	x2	4
y2	7	side_1	?	side_2	?
distance	?				

The values of variables that were not given initial values are unspecified, indicated by a question mark; sometimes these values are called **garbage values** because they are values left in memory from the previous program. A diagram such as this one, of a variable along with its identifier and its value, is called a **memory snapshot** because it shows the contents of a memory location at a specified point in the execution of a program. We frequently use memory snapshots of the contents of variables both before and after a statement is executed in order to show the effect of the statement.

The rules for selecting a valid identifier are summarized in the following list:

- An identifier must begin with an alphabetic character or the underscore character _.
- Alphabetic characters in an identifier can be lowercase or uppercase letters.
- An identifier can contain digits, but not as the first character.
- An identifier can be of any length.

C++ is **case sensitive**; that is, it distinguishes uppercase letters from lowercase letters. Thus, **Total**, **TOTAL**, and **total** represent three different variables. C++ also includes **keywords** with special meaning to the C++ compiler that cannot be used for identifiers; a complete list is given in Table 2.1.

Examples of valid identifiers are **distance**, **x_1**, **X_Sum**, **average_measurement**, and **initial_time**. Examples of invalid identifiers are **1x** (begins with a digit), **minimum-x** (contains an invalid character, -), **I/O** (contains an invalid character, /), **switch** (a keyword), **$sum** (contains an invalid character, $), and **rate%** (contains an invalid character, %).

Style

An identifier should be carefully selected so that it reflects the contents of the variable. *If possible, the name should also indicate the units of measurement.* For example, if a variable represents a temperature measurement in degrees Fahrenheit, use an identifier such as **temp_F** or **degrees_F**, or if a variable repre-

TABLE 2.1 Keywords

asm	double	new	switch
auto	else	operator	template
break	enum	private	this
case	extern	protected	throw
catch	float	public	try
char	for	register	typedef
class	friend	return	union
const	goto	short	unsigned
continue	if	signed	virtual
default	inline	sizeof	void
delete	int	static	volatile
do	long	struct	while

sents an angle, name it **theta_rad** to indicate that the angle is measured in radians or **theta_deg** to indicate that the angle is measured in degrees.

The declarations in the **main** function (and also in other C++ functions described in Chapter 4) not only must include all identifiers that we plan to use in our program, but also must specify the types of values that will be stored in the variables. These data types will be presented after a discussion on scientific notation. Note that we do not have to declare all variables at the beginning of the **main** function. We must, however, declare a variable before we use it. In the sample programs in this text, you will see that we often delay defining a variable so that the definition is near the statements that use it or so that it can be initialized with a value that must first be computed.

Practice!

Determine which of the following names are valid identifiers. If a name is not a valid identifier, give the reason that it is not, and suggest a valid replacement.

1. **xsum**	2. **x_sum**	3. **tax-rate**	4. **perimeter**
5. **sec^2**	6. **degrees_C**	7. **count**	8. **void**
9. **f(x)**	10. **m/s**	11. **Final_Value**	12. **w1.1**

SCIENTIFIC NOTATION

Floating-point

A **floating-point** value represents a real number, such as 2.5, -0.004, and 15.0. A real number is often expressed in **scientific notation** by rewriting it as a mantissa times a power of 10, where the **mantissa** has an absolute value greater than or equal to 1.0 and less than 10.0. For example, in scientific notation, 25.6 is written as 2.56×10^1, -0.004 is written as -4.0×10^{-3}, and 1.5 is written as 1.5×10^0. In **exponential notation**, the letter e is used to separate the mantissa from the exponent of the power of 10. Thus, in exponential notation, 25.6 is written as 2.56e1, -0.004 is written as $-4.0e-3$, and 1.5 is written as 1.5e0.

Precision

The number of digits allowed by the computer for the decimal portion of the mantissa determines the **precision** of the real number, and the number of digits allowed for the exponent determines its **range**. Thus, values with one digit of precision and a range for the exponent of -8 to 7 could include values such as 2.3×10^5 (230,000) and 5.9×10^{-8} (0.000000059). This precision and range would not be sufficient for many of the types of values that we use in solving engineering problems. For example, the distance in miles from Mars to the Sun, with seven digits of precision, is 141,517,510 or 1.4151751×10^8; to represent this value, we would need at least seven digits of precision and a range for the exponent that included the integer 8.

Practice!

In Problems 1–4, express the value in scientific notation and in exponential notation. Specify the number of digits of precision needed to represent each value.

1. 35.004   2. 0.00042   3. −0.0999   4. 10,000,002.8

In Problems 5–8, express the value as a real value.

5. 1.03e−5   6. −1.05e5   7. −3.552e6   8. 6.67e−4

NUMERIC DATA TYPES

Numeric data types are used to specify the types of numbers that will be contained in variables. In C++, numeric values are either integers or floating-point values, as shown in Figure 2.1. Nonnumeric data types (such as characters) are discussed in Chapter 6.

Type specifiers   The **type specifiers** for signed integers are **short**, **int**, and **long**, for short integer, integer, and long integer, respectively. The specific ranges of values are **system dependent**, which means that the ranges can vary from one system to another. On many systems, the short integer and the integer range from −32,768 to 32,767, while the long integer represents values from −2,147,483,648 to 2,147,483,647. (The unusual limits such as 32,767 and 2,147,483,647 relate to conversions of decimal values to binary for internal representation in the computer.)

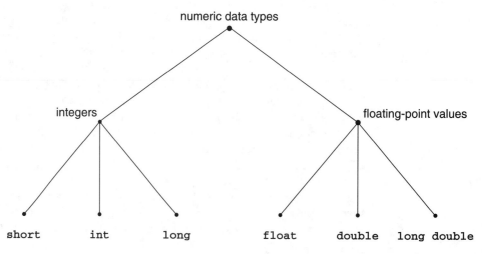

Figure 2.1 *Numeric data types.*

C++ also allows an **unsigned qualifier** to be added to integer specifiers, where an unsigned integer represents only positive values. Because unsigned integers do not need to represent the sign (positive or negative), the range of positive values is twice that of the corresponding signed integers. For example, if an unsigned short integer has the range of values from 0 to 65,535, then a short integer will have the range of values from −32,768 to 32,767; both variables can represent a total of 65,536 values.

The type specifiers for floating-point values are `float` (single precision), `double` (double precision), and `long double` (extended precision). The following statement from Program `chapter1_1` thus defines seven variables that all contain double-precision floating-point values:

```
double x1=1, y1=5, x2=4, y2=7,
       side_1, side_2, distance;
```

The difference between the `float`, `double`, and `long double` types relates to the precision (or accuracy) and range of the values represented. Both precision and range are system dependent. Table 2.2 contains information on the precision and range of integers and floating-point values used by the Borland C++ compiler, which can compile C programs as well. (Recall that C++ is an extension of C.) On most systems, a `double` data type stores about twice as many decimal digits of precision as are stored with a `float` data type. In addition, a `double` value will have a wider range of values for exponents than a `float` value. A `long double` value may have more precision and a still wider range for exponents. A floating-point constant such as 2.3 is assumed to be a `double` constant. To specify a `float` constant or a `long double` constant, the letter (or suffix) `F` or `L` must be appended to the constant. Thus, `2.3F` and `2.3L` represent a `float` constant and a `long double` constant, respectively.

TABLE 2.2 Example of Data Type Limits*	
Integers	
`short`	maximum = 32,767
`int`	maximum = 32,767
`long`	maximum = 2,147,483,647
Floating Point	
`float`	6 digits of precision maximum exponent = 38 maximum value = 3.402823e+38
`double`	15 digits of precision maximum exponent = 308 maximum value = 1.797693e+308
`long double`	19 digits of precision maximum exponent = 4932 maximum value = 1.189731e+4932

*Borland Turbo C++ 3.0 compiler

SYMBOLIC CONSTANTS

Style

A **symbolic constant** is declared by prefixing a declaration with the **const** specifier. The symbolic constant can appear anywhere in a C++ program; the compiler will replace each occurrence of the constant identifier with the constant value. *Engineering constants such as π or g, the acceleration due to gravity, are good candidates for symbolic constants.* For example, consider the following constant declaration to assign the value 3.141593 to the **double** identifier **PI**:

```
const double PI=3.141593;
```

Statements that need to use the value of π would then use the symbolic constant instead of 3.141593, as illustrated in the statement

```
area = PI*radius*radius;
```

which computes the area of a circle.

Style

Symbolic constants are usually defined with uppercase identifiers (as in **PI** *instead of* **pi**) *to indicate that they are symbolic constants, and of course, the identifiers should be selected so that they are easy to remember.* Finally, several symbolic constants can be declared in one statement if they have the same data type. Note that **const** declarations, like variable declarations, end with a semicolon.

In the next section, we discuss C++ statements that allow us to assign values to variables. These assignment statements could be used to assign constant values to variables, but we will see later that there are some special advantages to using symbolic constants in many cases.

Practice!

Give **const** declarations to assign symbolic constants for these constants:

1. speed of light, $c = 2.99792 \times 10^8$ m/s
2. charge of an electron, $e = 1.602177 \times 10^{-19}$ C
3. acceleration due to gravity, $g = 9.8$ m/s^2
4. acceleration due to gravity, $g = 32$ ft/s^2
5. radius of the moon, $r = 1.74 \times 10^6$ m

2.3   Assignment Statements

An **assignment statement** is used to assign a value to an identifier. The general form of the assignment statement is

```
identifier = expression;
```

Expression

where **expression** can be a constant, another variable, or the result of an operation. Consider the following two sets of statements that declare and give values to the variables **sum** and **x1**:

```
double sum=10.5;        double sum;
int x1=3;               int x1;
                          .
                          .
                          .
                        sum = 10.5;
                        x1 = 3;
```

After either set of statements is executed, the value of **sum** is 10.5 and the value of **x1** is 3, as shown in the following memory snapshot:

sum | 10.5 | x1 | 3 |

The assignment statements on the left define and initialize the variables at the same time; the assignment statements on the right could be used at any point in the program and thus may change (as opposed to initialize) the values in variables. Note that a symbolic constant (such as **PI**, defined in the last section) cannot be placed on the left side of an assignment statement because you cannot change its value in a program.

Multiple
assignments

Multiple assignments are also allowed in C++, as in the following statement, which assigns a value of zero to each of the variables **x**, **y**, and **z**:

```
x = y = z = 0;
```

Multiple assignments are discussed further at the end of this section.

We can also assign a value from one variable to another with an assignment statement:

```
rate = state_tax;
```

The equals sign should be read as "is assigned the value of"; thus, this statement says, "**rate** is assigned the value of **state_tax**." If **state_tax** contains the value 0.06, then **rate** will contain the value 0.06 after the statement is executed; the value in **state_tax** is not changed. The memory snapshots before and after the statement is executed are as follows:

Before: rate | ? | state_tax | 0.06 |

After: rate | 0.06 | state_tax | 0.06 |

If we assign a value of one data type to a variable of a different data type, then a conversion must occur during the execution of the statement. Sometimes the conversion can result in information being lost. For example, consider the following declaration and assignment statement:

```
int a;
      .
      .
      .
a = 12.8;
```

Since **a** is defined to be an integer, it cannot store a value with a nonzero decimal portion. Therefore, in this case, the memory snapshot after executing the assignment statement is as follows:

a | 12 |

Numeric conversion

To determine whether a **numeric conversion** will work properly, we use the following order, which is from high to low:

```
high:    long double
         double
         float
         long int
         int
low:     short int
```

If a value is moved to a data type that is higher in order, no information will be lost; if a value is moved to a data type that is lower in order, information may be lost. Thus, moving an **int** to a **double** will work properly, but moving a **float** to an **int** may result in the loss of some information or an incorrect result. (Note that unsigned integers are not included in the list because errors can occur in both directions.) In general, use only assignments that will not cause conversion problems.

ARITHMETIC OPERATORS

An assignment statement can be used to assign the result of an arithmetic operation to a variable, as shown in this statement, which computes the area of a square:

```
area_square = side*side;
```

(* is used to indicate multiplication.)

The symbols + and – are used to indicate addition and subtraction, and the symbol / is used for division. Thus, each of the following statements is a valid computation for the area of a triangle:

```
area_triangle = 0.5*base*height;
area_triangle = (base*height)/2;
```

The parentheses in the second statement are not required, but are used for readability.

Consider the assignment statement

```
x = x + 1;
```

In algebra, this statement is invalid because a value cannot be equal to itself plus 1. However, in C++ the statement should not be read as an equality; instead, it should be read as "**x** is assigned the value of **x**, plus 1." With this interpretation, the statement indicates that the value stored in the variable **x** is incremented by 1. Thus, if the value of **x** is 5 before the statement is executed, then the value of **x** will be 6 after the statement is executed.

Modulus operator

C++ also includes a **modulus operator**, **%**, which computes the remainder when one integer is divided by another. For example, **5%2** is equal to 1, **6%3** is equal to 0, and **2%7** is equal to 2. (The quotient of **2/7** is zero with a remainder of 2.) If **a** and **b** are integers, then the expression **a/b** computes the integer quotient, while the expression **a%b** computes the integer remainder. Hence, if **a** is equal to 9 and **b** is equal to 4, the value of **a/b** is 2 and the value of **a%b** is 1. An execution error occurs if the value of **b** is equal to zero in either **a/b** or **a%b** because the computer cannot perform division by zero. If either of the integer values in **a** and **b** are negative, the value of **a%b** is system dependent.

The modulus operator is useful in determining whether an integer is a multiple of another number. For example, if **a%2** is equal to zero, then **a** is even; otherwise **a** is odd. If **a%5** is equal to zero, then **a** is a multiple of 5. We will use the modulus operator frequently in the development of engineering solutions.

The five operators (**+, -, *, /,%**) discussed in the previous paragraphs are **binary operators**—operators that operate on two values. C++ also includes **unary operators**—operators that operate on a single value. For example, plus and minus signs are unary operators when they are used in an expression such as **-x**.

The result of a binary operation with values of the same type is another value of the same type. For example, if **a** and **b** are **double** values, then the result of **a/b** is also a **double** value. Similarly, if **a** and **b** are integers, then the result of **a/b** is also an integer. However, an integer division can sometimes produce unexpected results because any decimal portion of the integer division is dropped; the result is a **truncated result**, not a rounded result. Thus, **5/3** is equal to 1, and **3/6** is equal to 0.

Truncated result

An operation between values with different types is a **mixed operation.** Before the operation is performed, the value with the lower type is converted or promoted to the higher type (as discussed for conversions within assignment statements), and thus, the operation is performed with values of the same type. For example, if an operation is specified between an **int** and a **float**, the integer will be converted to a **float** before the operation is performed; the result will be a **float**.

Suppose that we want to compute the average of a set of integers. If the sum and the count of the integers have been stored in the integer variables **sum** and **count**, respectively, it would seem that the following statements should correctly compute the average:

```
int sum, count;
float average;
  .
  .
  .
average = sum/count;
```

Cast operator

However, the division between the two integers gives an integer result that is then converted to a `float`. Thus, if `sum` is 18 and `count` is 5, then the value of `average` is 3.0, not 3.6. To compute this sum correctly, we use a **cast operator**—a unary operator that allows us to specify a type change in the value before the next computation. In this example, let us apply the cast `(float)` to `sum` and `count`:

```
average = (float)sum/(float)count;
```

The values of `sum` and `count` are converted to `float` values before the division is performed. The result of the division is then a `float` that is stored in `average`. If the value of `sum` is 18 and the value of `count` is 5, the value of `average` is now correctly computed to be 3.6. Note that the cast operator affects only the value used in the computation; it does not change the values stored in the variables `sum` and `count`.

Practice!

Give the values computed by each of the following sets of statements:

1.
```
int a=27, b=6, c, d;
     .
     .
     .
c = a/b;
d = a%b;
```

2.
```
int a=27, b=6;
float c;
     .
     .
     .
c = a/(float)b;
```

3.
```
int a;
float b=6, c=18.6;
     .
     .
     .
a = c/b;
```

4.
```
int b=6;
float a, c=18.6;
     .
     .
     .
a = (int)c/b;
```

PRIORITY OF OPERATORS

Precedence

In an expression that contains more than one arithmetic operator, we need to be concerned about the order in which the operations are performed. Table 2.3 contains the **precedence** of the arithmetic operators, which matches their order of evaluation in algebra. Operations within parentheses are always evaluated first; if the parentheses are nested, the operations within the innermost parentheses are evaluated first. Unary operators are evaluated before the binary operators `*`, `/`, and `%`; binary addition and subtraction are evaluated last. If there are several operators with the same precedence in an expression, the variables or constants are grouped (or associated) together with the operators in a specific order, as specified in Table 2.3. For example, consider the expression

```
a*b + b/c*d
```

TABLE 2.3 Precedence of Arithmetic Operators		
Precedence	Operator	Associativity
1	parentheses: ( )	innermost first
2	unary operators: + - cast	right to left
3	binary operators: * / %	left to right
4	binary operators: + -	left to right

Associativity

Since multiplication and division have the same precedence, and since the **associativity** (the order for grouping the operations) is from left to right, this expression will be evaluated as if it were written

```
(a*b) + ((b/c)*d)
```

The order of precedence does not specify whether `a*b` is evaluated before `(b/c)*d`; in fact, the order of evaluation of these terms is system dependent.

Style

The spacing within an arithmetic expression is a style issue. Some people prefer to put spaces around each operator. We prefer to put spaces only around binary addition and subtraction, since they are evaluated last. *Choose the spacing style that you prefer, but then use it consistently.*

Suppose that we want to compute the area of a trapezoid and that we have declared four **double** variables: **base, height_1, height_2**, and **area**. Suppose further that the variables **base, height_1**, and **height_2** already have values. Then a statement that will correctly compute the area of the trapezoid is

```
area = 0.5*base*(height_1 + height_2);
```

If we omitted the parentheses in the expression, obtaining

```
area = 0.5*base*height_1 + height_2;
```

then the statement would be executed as if it were the statement

```
area = ((0.5*base)*height_1) + height_2;
```

Note that although an incorrect answer would be computed, there is no message to alert us to the error. Therefore, it is important to be very careful when converting expressions into C++. In general, use parentheses to indicate the order of operations in a complicated expression to avoid confusion and to be sure that the expression is evaluated in the manner desired.

You may have noticed that we have not listed any exponentiation operator to compute values such as x^4. A special mathematical function that performs exponentiation will be discussed later in the chapter. Of course, exponentiation with integer exponents, as in a^2, can be computed with repeated multiplications $a \times a$ (**a*a** in C++).

Style

Long expressions should be broken into several statements for evaluation. For example, consider the equation

$$f = \frac{x^3 - 2x^2 + x - 6.3}{x^2 + 0.05005x - 3.14}$$

If we try to evaluate this equation in one assignment statement, it becomes too long to be easily read:

```
f = (x*x*x - 2*x*x + x - 6.3)/(x*x + 0.05005*x - 3.14);
```

One solution is to break the statement into two lines:

```
f = (x*x*x - 2*x*x + x - 6.3)/
    (x*x + 0.05005*x - 3.14);
```

Another solution is to compute the numerator and denominator separately:

```
numerator = x*x*x - 2*x*x + x - 6.3;
denominator = x*x + 0.05005*x - 3.14;
f = numerator/denominator;
```

The variables x, numerator, denominator, and f must be floating-point variables in order to compute the correct value of f.

Practice!

In Problems 1 and 2, give C++ statements to compute the indicated values. Assume that the identifiers in the expressions have been defined as **double** variables and have been assigned appropriate values.

1. Tension in a cord:

$$\text{tension} = \frac{2m_1 m_2}{m_1 + m_2} g$$

where g is the acceleration due to gravity; that is,

$g = 9.80665$ m/s²

2. Fluid pressure at the end of a pipe:

$$P_2 = P_1 + \frac{\rho v_2^2 (A_2^2 - A_1^2)}{2A_1^2}$$

In Problems 3 and 4, give the mathematical equations computed by the C++ statements. Assume that the following symbolic constants have been defined:

```
const double PI=3.141593, G=6.67259e-11;
```

3.   Centripetal acceleration:

```
centripetal = 4*PI*PI*r/(T*T);
```

4.   Change in potential energy:

```
change = G*M_E*m*(1/R_E - 1/(R_E + h));
```

OVERFLOW AND UNDERFLOW

The values stored in a computer have a wide range of allowed values. However, if the result of a computation exceeds this range, an error occurs. For example, suppose that the range for the exponent of a floating-point value is from -38 to 38. This range should accommodate most computations, but it is possible for the results of an expression to be outside of it. For example, suppose that we execute the following commands:

```
x = 2.5e30;
y = 1.0e30;
z = x*y;
```

The values of x and y are within the allowable range. However, the value of z, should be 2.5e60, but this value exceeds the range. This error is called **exponent overflow** because the exponent of the result of an arithmetic operation is too large to store in the memory assigned to the variable. The action generated by an exponent overflow is system dependent.

Exponent underflow is a similar error caused by the exponent of the result of an arithmetic operation being too small to store in the memory assigned to the variable. Using the same allowable range as in the previous example, we obtain an exponent underflow with the following commands:

```
x = 2.5e-30;
y = 1.0e30;
z = x/y;
```

Here again, the values of x and y are within the allowable range, but the correct value of z, $2.5e-60$, is not. Because the exponent is less than the minimum value allowed, we have caused an exponent underflow. As with an overflow, the action generated by an exponent underflow is system dependent; on some systems, the result will automatically be zero. Using double precision or extended precision can help avoid problems with exponent overflow or underflow, although this does not completely solve the problem, since there will always be a finite range.

INCREMENT AND DECREMENT OPERATORS

The C++ language contains unary operators for incrementing and decrementing variables; these operators cannot be used with constants or expressions. The **increment operator ++** and the **decrement operator --** can be applied either in a

prefix position (before the identifier) as in ++count, or in a **postfix position** (after the identifier), as in count++. If an increment or decrement operator is used with a variable alone, it is equivalent to an assignment statement that increments or decrements the variable. Thus, the statement

```
y--;
```

is equal to the statement

```
y = y - 1;
```

If an increment or decrement operator is used in an expression, then the expression must be evaluated carefully. If the increment or decrement operator is in a prefix position, the identifier is modified, and then the new value is used in evaluating the rest of the expression. If the increment or decrement operator is in a postfix position, the old value of the identifier is used to evaluate the rest of the expression, and then the identifier is modified. Thus, the statement

```
w = ++x - y;
```
(2.1)

is equivalent to the pair of statements

```
x = x + 1;
w = x - y;
```

while the statement

```
w = x++ - y;
```
(2.2)

is equivalent to the pair of statements

```
w = x - y;
x = x + 1;
```

When executing either (2.1) or (2.2), if we assume that the value of x is equal to 5 and the value of y is equal to 3, then the value of x increases to 6. However, after executing (2.1), the value of w is 3, but after executing (2.2), the value of w is 2.

The increment and decrement operators have the same precedence as the other unary operators. If several unary operators are in an expression, they are associated from right to left.

ABBREVIATED ASSIGNMENT OPERATORS

C++ allows simple assignment statements that modify the value of a variable to be abbreviated. For example, each of the following pairs contains equivalent statements:

```
x = x + 3;
x += 3;
```

```
sum = sum + x;
sum += x;

d = d/4.5;
d /= 4.5;

r = r%2;
r %= 2;
```

In fact, any statement of the form

identifier = identifier operator expression;

can be written in the form

identifier operator = expression;

Abbreviated assignment statements are often used in place of their longer counterparts because they are shorter.

Earlier in this section, we used the multiple-assignment statement

```
x = y = z = 0;
```

The interpretation of this statement is clear, but the interpretation of the following statement is not as evident:

```
a = b += c + d;
```

To evaluate this statement properly, we use Table 2.4, which indicates that the assignment operators are evaluated last and their associativity is from right to left. Thus, the statement is equivalent to

```
a = (b += (c + d));
```

If we replace the abbreviated forms with the longer forms of the operations, we have

```
a = (b = b + (c + d));
```

or

```
b = b + (c + d);
a = b;
```

Evaluating this statement by means of Table 2.4 is good practice, but in general, statements used in a program should be more readable. Therefore, using abbreviated assignment statements in a multiple-assignment statement is not recommended. *Also, note that the spacing conventions that we use insert spaces around abbreviated operators and multiple-assignment operators because these operators are evaluated after the arithmetic operators.*

Abbreviated assignment

Style

Precedence	Operator	Associativity
	TABLE 2.4 Precedence of Arithmetic and Assignment Operators	
1	parentheses: `( )`	innermost first
2	unary operators: `+ - ++ -- cast`	right to left
3	binary operators: `* / %`	left to right
4	binary operators: `+ -`	left to right
5	assignment operators: `= += -= *= /= %=`	right to left

Practice!

Give a memory snapshot after each statement is executed, assuming that **x** is equal to 2 and that **y** is equal to 4 before the statement is executed. Assume that all the variables are integers.

1. `z = x++*y;`

2. `z = ++x*y;`

3. `x += y;`

4. `y %= x;`

2.4   Standard Input and Output

Thus far, we have discussed statements for declaring variables and then using the variables to compute new values. We now present a statement that allows us to print the new values computed. In addition, we discuss a statement that allows us to enter values from the keyboard when a program is executed. To use either of these statements in a program, we must include the preprocessor directive

```
#include <iostream.h>
```

This directive gives the compiler the information that it needs to check references to the input/output functions in the Standard C++ library.

cout STATEMENT

The **cout** statement allows us to print values and explanatory text to the screen. For example, consider the following statement, which prints the value of a variable named **angle** along with the corresponding units:

```
cout << "angle = " << angle << " radians" << endl;
```

Control strings   The insertion operator `<<` inserts information in the form of **control strings** (enclosed in double quotes) or variable expressions into an output stream of information that is is displayed on the screen when the **endl** (end line) reference is encountered. In this example, the **<<** operators insert the information in the first control string into the output stream, inserts the value of the variable **angle** into the output stream, and insert the correct units into the output stream; then, the combined stream of information is displayed on the screen. If the value of **angle** is 2.841214, then the output generated by the statement is

```
angle = 2.841214 radians
```

Style

In engineering, it is very important to include the corresponding units in the output along with the numerical values.

If a **cout** statement is long, you should split it into several lines, choosing a split that preserves readability. For example, a good split is generally before the operator and its accompanying control string or expression. To split a control string, break the text into two separate pieces of text, each in its own set of quotation marks. The following statements show several different ways to print the same output line:

```
cout << "distance between the points is "
     << distance << endl;

cout << "distance between the "
     <<  "points is " << distance << endl;

cout << "distance between the points is ";
cout << distance << endl;

cout << "distance between the ";
cout <<  "points is " << distance << endl;
```

Note the differences between splitting one long **cout** statement into several lines and rewriting the long **cout** statement as two short **cout** statements.

Escape character

The backslash (\) is called an **escape character** when it is used in a control string. The compiler combines it with the character that follows it and then attaches a special meaning to the resulting combination of characters. The sequence \\ is used to insert a single backslash in a control string, and the sequence \" will insert a double quote in a control string. Thus, the output of the statement

```
cout << "\"The End.\"" << endl;
```

is

```
"The End."
```

The other **escape sequences** recognized by C++ are given in Table 2.5.

FORMATTED OUTPUT FUNCTIONS

Manipulators

The Standard C++ library contains **format functions**—usually called **manipulators**—that can be used with the **cout** statement. For example, we can use the **setw** function to set the **field width** (the number of character positions that a number

TABLE 2.5 Escape Sequences

Sequence	Character Represented
\a	alert (bell) character
\b	backspace
\f	form feed
\n	new line
\r	carriage return
\t	horizontal tab
\v	vertical tab
\\	backslash
\?	question mark
\'	single quote
\"	double quote

will occupy on the screen) for the next value that is displayed. The basic form of the **setw** manipulator is

```
setw(size)
```

This function contains one integer argument that specifies the number of characters to use in displaying the next value. For example, the following statement prints the value of **x** in a field of eight spaces:

```
cout << setw(8) << x;
```

The field width will be increased, if necessary, to more than eight spaces to print the value that is output. If the field width specifies more positions than are needed for the value, the value is right justified, which means that the extra positions to the left of the value are filled with blanks.

Note that the **setw** manipulator only specifies the field width for the next item in the **cout** statement. After that item is displayed, the field width reverts to the default value of 0. Therefore, the statement

```
cout << setw(10) << x << y;
```

only displays the value of **x** in a field that is 10 characters wide. The value of **y**, however, uses just enough space to display it completely.

The **setprecision** manipulator can be used to specify the precision of a value to be displayed (the number of digits after the decimal point). The basic form of the **setprecision** manipulator is

```
setprecision(digit)
```

where the argument of the function is an integer indicating the number of digits after the decimal point. For example, the statement

```
cout << setprecision(2) << setw(8) << x;
```

prints the value of **x** with two digits after the decimal point, using a total field width of eight spaces. The decimal portion of a value is rounded to the specified precision; thus, the value 14.51578 of **x** will be printed as 14.52, with three blanks to its left. The **setprecision** manipulator is applied to all subsequent output.

TABLE 2.6 Common Manipulators	
Manipulator	**Description**
`setw(size)`	sets the field width
`setprecision(digit)`	sets the precision
`setfill(char)`	fills the field with the character
`ws`	removes white spaces

The preprocessor directive

```
#include <iomanip.h>
```

must be inserted in a program if we plan to use a manipulator. Table 2.6 describes the commonly used manipulators.

Practice!

Assume that the integer variable **sum** contains the value 150 and that the **double** variable **average** contains the value 12.368. Show the output line (or lines) generated by the following statements.

1.
```
cout << "sum = " << sum << endl << endl
     << "average = " << average << endl;
```

2.
```
cout << "sum and average" << endl;
cout << sum << setw(8) << setprecision(2)
     << average << endl;
```

3.
```
cout << setprecision(2) << average
     << " is the average;" << endl;
cout << sum << " is the sum" << endl;
```

4.
```
cout << setprecision(2) << average
     << " is the average; ";
cout << setw(6) << sum << " is the sum" << endl;
```

cin STATEMENT

The **cin** statement allows us to enter values from the keyboard when a program is executed. For example, suppose that a program computes the number of acres of new forest growth after a specified period of time elapses. If the time elapsed is a constant in the program, we would have to change the value of the constant and then recompile and reexecute the program to obtain the output for a different period. Alternatively, if we use the **cin** statement to read the period, we do not need to recompile the program; we only need to reexecute it and enter the desired period from the keyboard.

For instance, if the value to be entered through the keyboard is an integer that is to be stored in the variable **year**, we could use the following **cin** statement to read the value:

```
cin >> year;
```

Input operator

Here, **>>** is called the **input operator**. Since C++ supports the input of each standard data type (integer, floating point, and character), we can use the **>>** operator to obtain the input of any value from the keyboard. When we need multiple input values, the order of operations is simple: The first variable mentioned is input first, and the others are input in the order of their appearance, regardless of the data type involved. To illustrate, if we wish to read more than one value from the keyboard, we can use a **cin** statement with cascaded **>>** operators as follows:

```
int year;
double acres;
   .
   .
   .
cin >> acres >> year;
```

When the **cin** statement is executed, the program will read two values from the keyboard and convert them, in turn, into a **double** value and an **int** value. To help distinguish the input operator **>>** from the insertion operator **<<**, remember that the former directs the information toward the variable names for input and the latter directs the information toward the function name **cout** for output.

Style

To prompt the program user to enter the input values, a **cin** *statement is usually preceded by a* **cout** *statement that describes the information the user should enter from the keyboard:*

```
cout << "Enter the acres of forest "
        "and the period (years):" << endl;
cin >> acres >> year;
```

The **cout** statement ends with a new-line specifier, so the values entered by the user will be on the line (or lines) following the prompt text. Thus, after the previous statements are executed and the user has responded to the prompt, the information on the screen might be

```
Enter the acres of forest and the period (years):
15.5   10
```

or

```
Enter the acres of forest and the period (years):
15.5
10
```

2.5   Mathematical Functions

Arithmetic expressions that solve engineering problems often require computations other than addition, subtraction, multiplication, and division. For example, many expressions require the use of exponentiation, logarithms, exponentials, and trigonometric functions. In this section, we discuss the mathematical functions that are available in the **Standard C++ library**. The following preprocessor directive should be used in programs referencing these mathematical functions:

Standard C++ library

```
#include <math.h>
```

This directive specifies that information is to be added to the program to aid the compiler when it converts references to the mathematical functions in the Standard C++ library.

Before we discuss the rules relating to functions, let us consider a specific example. The following statement computes the sine of an angle **theta** and stores the result in the variable **b**:

```
b = sin(theta);
```

The **sin** function assumes that the argument is in radians. If the variable **theta** contains a value in degrees, we can convert the value to radians with a separate statement (recall that $180° = \pi$ radians):

```
const double PI=3.141593;
   .
   .
   .
theta_rad = theta*PI/180;
b = sin(theta_rad);
```

The conversion also can be specified within the function reference:

```
b = sin(theta*PI/180);
```

Performing the conversion with a separate statement is usually preferable because it is easier to understand.

A function reference, such as **sin(theta)**, represents a single value. The parentheses following the function name contain the inputs to the function, which are called **parameters** or **arguments**. A function may contain no arguments, one argument, or many arguments, depending on its definition. If a function contains more than one argument, it is very important to list the arguments in the correct order. Some functions also require that the arguments be in specific units. For example, the trigonometric functions assume that arguments are in radians. Most of the mathematical functions assume that the arguments are **double** values; if a different type of argument is used, it is converted to **double** before the function is executed.

Arguments

A function reference can be part of the argument of another function reference. For example, the following statement computes the logarithm of the absolute value of **x**:

```
b = log(fabs(x));
```

When one function is used to compute the argument of another function, be sure to enclose the argument of each function in its own set of parentheses. This nesting of functions is also called **composition** of functions.

We next discuss several categories of functions commonly used in engineering computations. Other functions will be presented throughout the remaining chapters as we discuss subjects relevant to them. Tables of common functions are included on the last two pages of the book for easy reference.

ELEMENTARY MATHEMATICAL FUNCTIONS

The elementary mathematical functions include functions that perform a number of common computations such as computing the absolute value of a number and computing the square root of a number. In addition, they include a group of functions used to perform rounding. These functions assume that the type of each argument is **double**, and the functions all return a **double**; if an argument is not a **double**, a conversion will occur using the rules described in Section 2.3. Following are the elementary mathematical functions with a brief description of each:

fabs(x)	This function computes the absolute value of x.
sqrt(x)	This function computes the square root of x. Errors occur if $x < 0$.
pow(x,y)	This function is used for exponentiation and computing the value of x to the y power, or x^y. Errors occur if $x = 0$ and $y \leq 0$, or if $x < 0$ and y is not an integer.
ceil(x)	This functions rounds x up to the nearest integer towards infinity (∞). For example, **ceil(2.01)** is equal to 3.
floor(x)	This function rounds x down to the nearest integer towards negative infinity ($-\infty$). For example, **floor(2.01)** is equal to 2.
exp(x)	This function computes the value of e^x, where e is the base for natural logarithms, or approximately 2.718282.
log(x)	This function returns ln x, the natural logarithm of x to the base e. Errors occur if $x \leq 0$.
log10(x)	This function returns $\log_{10}x$, the common logarithm of x to the base 10. Errors occur if $x \leq 0$.

Remember that the logarithm of a negative value or zero does not exist, and thus, an execution error occurs if you use a logarithm function with a negative or zero value for its argument.

An additional mathematical function that you may find useful is the **abs** function. This function computes the absolute value of an integer and returns an integer value. The header file containing information relative to the function is **stdlib.h**, and it should be included in programs referencing **abs**.

Practice!

Evaluate the following expressions:

1. `floor(-2.6)`
2. `ceil(-2.6)`
3. `pow(2,-3)`
4. `sqrt(floor(10.7))`

TRIGONOMETRIC FUNCTIONS

The trigonometric functions assume that all their arguments are of type `double`, and they return values of type `double`. In addition, as previously stated, the trigonometric functions assume that angles are represented in radians. To convert radians to degrees or degrees to radians, use the following conversions, which are based on the fact that $180° = \pi$ radians:

```
const double PI=3.141593;
    .
    .
    .
angle_deg = angle_rad*(180/PI);
angle_rad = angle_deg*(PI/180);
```

The trigonometric functions are included in the Standard C++ library, and a preprocessor directive including the information in `math.h` should be used with these functions. Following is a brief summary of the trigonometric functions:

`sin(x)`	This function computes the sine of x, where x is in radians.
`cos(x)`	This function computes the cosine of x, where x is in radians.
`tan(x)`	This function computes the tangent of x, where x is in radians.
`asin(x)`	This function computes the arcsine or inverse sine of x, where x must be in the range $[-1,1]$. The function returns an angle in radians in the range $[-\pi/2,\pi/2]$.
`acos(x)`	This function computes the arccosine or inverse cosine of x, where x must be in the range $[-1,1]$. The function returns an angle in radians in the range $[0,\pi]$.
`atan(x)`	This function computes the arctangent or inverse tangent of x. The function returns an angle in radians in the range $[-\pi/2,\pi/2]$.
`atan2(y,x)`	This function computes the arctangent or inverse tangent of the value y/x. The function returns an angle in radians in the range $[-\pi,\pi]$.

Note that the **atan** function always returns an angle in Quadrant I or IV, whereas the **atan2** function returns an angle that can be in any quadrant, depending on the signs of **x** and **y**. Thus, in many applications, the **atan2** function is preferred over the **atan** function. Note also that the inverse sine and inverse cosine are valid only for arguments in the interval $[-1,1]$.

Practice!

In Problems 1 and 2, give assignment statements for computing the indicated values, assuming that the variables have been declared and given appropriate values.

1. Length contraction, according to Einstein's special theory of relativity:

$$\text{length} = k\sqrt{1 - \left(\frac{v}{c}\right)^2}$$

2. Distance of the center of gravity from a reference plane in a sector of a hollow cylinder:

$$\text{center} = \frac{38.1972(r^3 - s^3)\sin a}{(r^2 - s^2)a}$$

In Problems 3 and 4, give the equation that corresponds to the assignment statement. Assume that the following declaration has been made:

```
const double g=9.8;
```

3. Range of a projectile:

```
range = (v0*v0/g)*sin(2*theta);
```

4. Speed of a disk at the bottom of an incline:

```
v = sqrt(2*g*h/(1 + I/(m*pow(r,2))));
```

2.6   Problem Solving Applied: Velocity Computation

In this section, we perform computations in an application related to the grand challenge of vehicle performance. An advanced turboprop engine called the **unducted fan** (UDF) is one of the promising new propulsion technologies being developed for future transport aircraft. Turboprop engines, which have been in use for decades, combine the power and reliability of jet engines with the efficiency of propellers. They are a significant improvement over earlier piston-powered propeller engines. Their application has been limited to smaller commuter-type

Unducted fan

aircraft, however, because they are not as fast or powerful as the fanjet engines used on larger airliners. The UDF engine employs significant advancements in propeller technology, which narrow the performance gap between turboprops and fanjets. New materials, new blade shapes, and higher rotation speeds enable UDF-powered aircraft to fly almost as fast as fanjets and with greater fuel efficiency. The UDF is also significantly quieter than the conventional turboprop.

During a test flight of a UDF-powered aircraft, the pilot has set the engine power level at 40,000 newtons (N), which causes the 20,000-kg aircraft to attain a cruise speed of 180 meters per second (m/s). The engine throttles are then set to a power level of 60,000 N, and the aircraft begins to accelerate. As the speed of the plane increases, the aerodynamic drag increases in proportion to the square of the speed. Eventually, the aircraft reaches a cruising speed such that the thrust from the UDF engines is just offset by the drag. The equations used to estimate the velocity and acceleration of the aircraft from the time that the throttle is reset until the plane reaches its cruising speed (at approximately 120 seconds (s)) are as follows:

$$\text{velocity} = 0.00001\ \text{time}^3 - 0.00488\ \text{time}^2 + 0.75795\ \text{time} + 181.3566$$
$$\text{acceleration} = 3 - 0.000062\ \text{velocity}^2$$

Plots of these functions are shown in Figure 2.2. Note that the acceleration approaches zero as the velocity approaches the cruising speed.

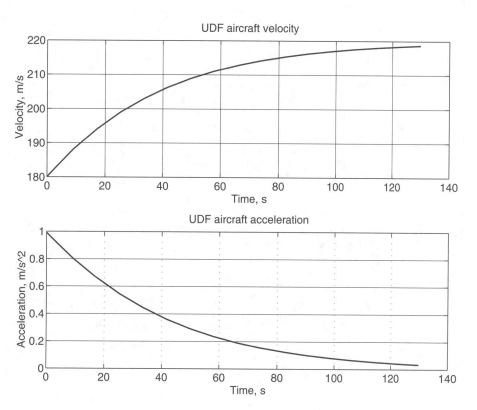

Figure 2.2 *UDF aircraft velocity and acceleration.*

Write a program that asks the user to enter the time elapsed (in seconds) since the power level was increased. Compute and print the corresponding acceleration and velocity of the aircraft at the new value of time.

1.   PROBLEM STATEMENT

Compute the new velocity and acceleration of the aircraft after a change in power level.

2.   INPUT/OUTPUT DESCRIPTION

The following diagram shows that the input to the program is a time value and that the output of the program is the pair of new velocity and acceleration values.

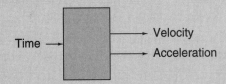

3.   HAND EXAMPLE

Suppose that the new time value is 50 s. Using a calculator and the equations given for the velocity and acceleration, we can compute

velocity = 208.3 m/s

acceleration = 0.31 m/s^2

4.   ALGORITHM DEVELOPMENT

The first step in the development of an algorithm is the decomposition of the solution to the problem into a set of sequentially executed steps:

Decomposition Outline:
1.   *Read new time value.*
2.   *Compute corresponding velocity and acceleration values.*
3.   *Print new velocity and acceleration.*

Because this program is very simple, we can convert the decomposition directly to C++:

```
//----------------------------------------------------------
//   Program chapter2_1
//
//   This program estimates new velocity and
//   acceleration values for a specified time.

#include <iostream.h>
#include <iomanip.h>
#include <stdlib.h>
#include <math.h>

int main()
{
    //   Define variables.
    double time, velocity, acceleration;

    //   Get time value from the keyboard.
    cout << "Enter new time value in seconds: ";
    cin >> time;

    //   Compute velocity and acceleration.
    velocity = 0.00001*pow(time,3) - 0.00488*pow(time,2)
               + 0.75795*time + 181.3566;
    acceleration = 3 - 0.000062*velocity*velocity;

    //   Print velocity and acceleration.
    cout << "velocity = " << setprecision(3)
         << velocity << " m/s" << endl;
    cout << "acceleration = " << setprecision(3)
         << acceleration << " m/s^2" << endl;

    //   Exit program.
    return EXIT_SUCCESS;
}
//----------------------------------------------------------
```

5.   TESTING

We first test the program using the data from the hand example. This generates the following output:

```
Enter new time value in seconds: 50
velocity = 208.304 m/s
acceleration = 0.31 m/s^2
```

Because the computed values match those of the hand example, we can test the program with other time values. If the values did not match, we would need to determine whether the error was in the hand example or in the program.

CHAPTER SUMMARY

In this chapter, we presented the C++ statements necessary to write simple programs that compute and print new values. We also presented the statement that allows us to enter information through the keyboard when the program is executing. The computations that were presented included the standard arithmetic operations, plus a large number of functions that can be used to perform the types of computations needed for engineering solutions.

KEY TERMS

abbreviated assignment
argument
assignment statement
associativity
binary operator
cast operator
comment
composition
constant
control string
declaration
decrement operator
escape sequence
exponential notation
expression
field width
floating-point value
format function
garbage value
identifier
increment operator
input operator
insertion operator

keyword
manipulator
mantissa
memory snapshot
modulus
multiple assignment
overflow
parameter
precedence
precision
preprocessor directive
prompt
range
scientific notation
Standard C++ library
statement
symbolic constant
system dependent
truncate
type specifier
unary operator
underflow
variable

C++ STATEMENT SUMMARY

Preprocessor directives to include information from the files in the Standard C++ Library:

```
#include <iostream.h>
#include <iomanip.h>
#include <stdlib.h>
#include <math.h>
```

Declarations for symbolic constants:

```
const double PI=3.141593;
const int PEOPLE=50;
```

Definitions for integers:

```
short sum=0;
int year_1, year_2;
long k;
```

Definitions for floating-point values:

```
float height_1, height_2;
double length=10, side1, side2;
long double distance, velocity;
```

Assignment statement:

```
area = 0.5*base*(height_1 + height_2);
```

Keyboard input statement:

```
cin >> year;
```

Screen output statement:

```
cout << "area is " << area
     << " square feet" << endl;
```

Program exit statement:

```
return EXIT_SUCCESS;
```

$\mathcal{STYLE}$ Notes

1. Use comments throughout a program to improve its readability and to document the steps in it.
2. If a long statement is broken into several lines, indent the lines following the first line.
3. Use blank lines to make a program more readable.
4. Use the units in a variable name whenever possible.
5. Symbolic constants should be used for engineering constants such as π.
6. Symbolic constants should generally be uppercase so that they are easily identified.
7. Use consistent spacing around arithmetic and assignment operators.
8. Use parentheses in complicated expressions to improve their readability and reduce the chance of errors.
9. To evaluate long expressions, break them into several statements.
10. Be sure to include units along with numerical values in the output of a program.
11. Use a prompt to the user to describe the information and units for values to be entered from the keyboard.

Debugging Notes

1. There is no space between < (or >) and the file name in an **include** directive.
2. Preprocessor directives do not end with a semicolon.
3. Declarations and statements must end with a semicolon.
4. Constant declarations must end with a semicolon.
5. A symbolic constant cannot be placed on the left side of an assignment statement.
6. If possible, avoid assignments that could cause information to be lost.
7. Use parentheses in a long expression to be sure that it is evaluated as desired.
8. Use double precision or extended precision to avoid problems with exponent overflow or underflow.
9. In nested function references, each set of arguments must be in its own set of parentheses.
10. Remember that the logarithm functions cannot be used with negative or zero values for arguments.
11. Be sure to use angles in radians with the trigonometric functions.
12. Remember that the inverse sine and inverse cosine functions have restrictions on their range of allowable input values.

PROBLEMS

Conversions. This set of problems involves conversions of a value in one unit to another unit. Each program should prompt the user for a value in the specified unit and then print the converted value along with the new unit.

1. Write a program to convert miles (mi) to kilometers (km). (Recall that 1 mi = 1.6093440 km.)

2. Write a program to convert pounds (lb) to kilograms (kg). (Recall that 1 kg has a weight of 2.205 lb.)

3. Write a program that converts degrees Fahrenheit (T_F) to degrees Rankine (T_R). (Recall that $T_F = T_R - 459.67$.)

4. Write a program to convert a speed in mi/hr to ft/s.

5. Write a program to compute the number of minutes necessary to cover a distance in miles if a car is traveling at 50 mi/hr.

Areas and Volumes. These problems involve computing an area or a volume with input from the user. Each program should include a prompt to the user to enter the variables needed.

6. Write a program to compute the area of a triangle with base b and height h. (Recall that $A = \frac{1}{2}bh$.)

7. Write a program to compute the area of a sector of a circle, where d is the angle in degrees between the radii. (Recall that $A = r^2\theta/2$, where θ is the angle in radians.)

8. Write a program to compute the volume of a sphere of radius r. (Recall that $V = \frac{4}{3}\pi r^3$.)

9. Write a program to read the radius of a sphere in inches, and then compute and print the surface area of the sphere in sq. ft. (Recall that the surface area of a sphere is $4\pi r^2$.)

10. Write a program to read the height and radius of a right circular cone. Then compute and print the height of a right circular cylinder with the same base and the same volume. (Recall that the volume of a right circular cone is $\frac{1}{3}Bh$, and that the volume of a circular cylinder is Bh, where B is the area of the base and h is the height.)

Molecular Weights of Amino Acids. The amino acids in proteins are composed of atoms of oxygen (O), carbon (C), nitrogen (N), sulfur (S), and hydrogen (H), as shown in Table 2.7. The molecular weights of the individual elements are as follows:

TABLE 2.7 Amino Acid Molecules

Amino Acid	O	C	N	S	H
Alanine	2	3	1	0	7
Arginine	2	6	4	0	15
Asparagine	3	4	2	0	8
Aspartic	4	4	1	0	6
Cysteine	2	3	1	1	7
Glutamic	4	5	1	0	8
Glutamine	3	5	2	0	10
Glycine	2	2	1	0	5
Histidine	2	6	3	0	10
Isoleucine	2	6	1	0	13
Leucine	2	6	1	0	13
Lysine	2	6	2	0	15
Methionine	2	5	1	1	11
Phenylalanine	2	9	1	0	11
Proline	2	5	1	0	10
Serine	3	3	1	0	7
Threonine	3	4	1	0	9
Tryptophan	2	11	2	0	11
Tyrosine	3	9	1	0	11
Valine	2	5	1	0	11

Element	Atomic Weight
O	15.9994
C	12.011
N	14.00674
S	32.066
H	1.00794

11. Write a program that asks the user to enter the number of atoms of each of the five elements for an amino acid. Then compute and print the molecular weight for this amino acid.

12. Write a program that asks the user to enter the number of atoms of each of the five elements for an amino acid. Then compute and print the average weight of the atoms in the amino acid.

13. Write a program to compute the molecular weight of cysteine. Then compute and print the percentage of the molecular weight that is due to carbon. Perform the computation so that the percentage is a value between 0 and 100, and print it with one decimal place as in 3.5 percent.

14. Write a program to compute the molecular weights of arginine and phenylalanine. Compute and print the absolute value of the difference in molecular weights for the two amino acids.

Logarithms to the Base b. To compute the logarithm of x to the base b, we can use the relationship

$$\log_b x = \frac{\log_e x}{\log_e b}$$

15. Write a program that reads a positive number and then computes and prints the logarithm of the value to the base 2. For example, the logarithm of 8 to the base 2 is 3, since $2^3 = 8$.

16. Write a program that reads a positive number and then computes and prints the logarithm of the value to the base 8. For example, the logarithm of 64 to the base 8 is 2, since $8^2 = 64$.

2

3

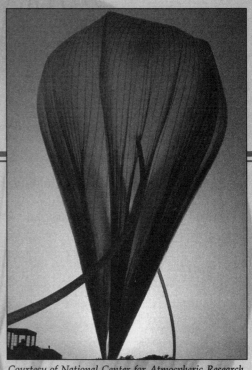

Courtesy of National Center for Atmospheric Research.

GRAND CHALLENGE:
Global Change

Weather balloons are used to collect data from the upper atmosphere. The balloons are filled with helium and rise to an equilibrium point at which the difference between the density of the helium inside the balloon and the density of the air outside the balloon is just enough to support the weight of the balloon. During the day, the Sun warms the balloon, causing it to rise to a new equilibrium point; in the evening, the balloon cools, and it descends to a lower altitude. The balloon can be used to measure the temperature, pressure, humidity, chemical concentration, and other properties of the air. A weather balloon may stay aloft for only a few hours or as long as several years collecting environmental data. The balloon falls back to earth as the helium leaks out or is released into the atmosphere.

Control Structures and Data Files

OBJECTIVES

In this chapter, we present structured programming in terms of sequence, selection, and repetition structures. After defining these structures using pseudocode and flowcharts, we discuss the C++ statements for implementing the structures. Sequence structures do not require new statements. The selection structure requires conditional expressions and `if` statements in order to provide alternative paths in a program. The repetition structure is implemented with three different loop structures: `while` loops, `do/while` loops, and `for` loops. An example that applies to weather balloons is used to illustrate conditional statements and loops. We also introduce simple data files at this point, because they are commonly used in solving engineering problems.

3.1   Development of Algorithms

In Chapter 2, the C++ programs that we developed were very simple. The steps were sequential and typically involved reading information from the keyboard, computing new information, and then printing the new information. Solving engineering problems, however, requires more complicated steps, and thus, we need to expand the part of our problem-solving process that deals with the development of algorithms.

TOP-DOWN DESIGN

A "big picture" description of the process of solving a problem with sequential logic is developed using **top-down design**. This overall description of the problem is refined until the steps are detailed enough to translate into statements in a programming language.

Decomposition Outline. We used **decomposition outlines** in Chapters 1 and 2 to sketch, in a rough manner, the solution to a problem. A decomposition outline is written sequentially and represents an ordered set of steps. For very simple problems, such as the one on page 50 of Chapter 2, we can go directly from the decomposition outline to C++ statements. However, for most problems, we need to refine the decomposition outline into a description with more detail. This process is often referred to as a **divide-and-conquer** strategy, since we keep breaking the solution to the problem into smaller and smaller portions.

Stepwise refinement

Stepwise Refinement. We call the breaking down of an outline into more detailed steps the **stepwise refinement** of the outline. Stepwise refinement can be done with pseudocode or a flowchart. **Pseudocode** uses English-like statements to describe the steps in an algorithm; a **flowchart** uses a diagram to do the same. The fundamental steps in most algorithms are shown in Figure 3.1, along with the corresponding notation in pseudocode and flowcharts.

Pseudocode and flowcharts are tools to help us determine the order of the steps we require to solve a problem. Both are commonly used, although not generally with the same problem. Sometimes we need to go through several levels of pseudocode or flowcharts to develop a solution to a complex problem. Decomposition outlines, pseudocode, and flowcharts are all models of the solution. Each person working on a solution will have different decomposition outlines and different pseudocode or flowcharts, just as the C++ programs developed by different people will be somewhat different, although they solve the same problem.

STRUCTURED PROGRAMMING

A structured program is a program that is written using simple control structures to organize the solution to a problem. A simple structure is usually defined to be a sequence, a selection, or a repetition. A **sequence** structure contains steps that are performed one after another. A **selection** structure contains one set of steps that is performed if a condition is true and another set of steps that is performed if the condition is false. A **repetition** structure contains a set of steps that

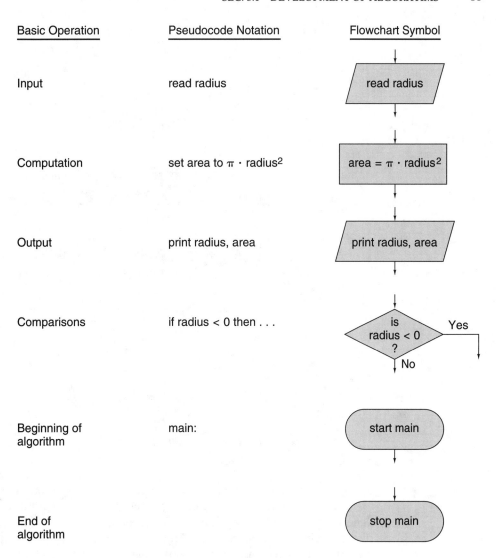

Basic Operation	Pseudocode Notation	Flowchart Symbol
Input	read radius	read radius
Computation	set area to $\pi \cdot$ radius^2	area = $\pi \cdot$ radius^2
Output	print radius, area	print radius, area
Comparisons	if radius < 0 then . . .	is radius < 0 ? Yes No
Beginning of algorithm	main:	start main
End of algorithm		stop main

Figure 3.1 *Pseudocode notation and flowchart symbols.*

is repeated as long as a condition is true. We next discuss each of these simple structures, using pseudocode and flowcharts to give specific examples.

Sequence. A sequence contains steps that are performed one after another. All the programs presented in Chapters 1 and 2 have a sequence structure. For example, the flowchart for the program that computed the velocity and acceleration of the aircraft with the UDF engine in Section 2.6 is shown in Figure 3.2.

Condition   **Selection.** A selection structure contains a **condition** that can be evaluated as either true or false. If the condition is true, then one set of statements is executed; if the condition is false, then another set of statements is executed. For

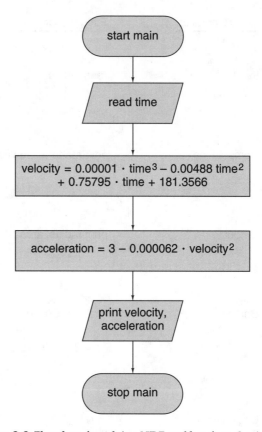

Figure 3.2 *Flowchart for solving UDF problem from Section 2.6.*

example, suppose that we have computed values for the numerator and denominator of a fraction. Before we compute the division, we want to be sure that the denominator is not close to zero. Therefore, the condition that we want to test is "denominator close to zero." If the condition is true, then we print a message indicating that we cannot compute the value. If the condition is false, which means that the denominator is not close to zero, then we compute and print the value of the fraction. In defining this condition, we need to state what we mean by "close to zero." For this example, we will assume that "close to zero" means that the absolute value of the denominator is less than 0.0001. Following is a description, in pseudocode, of the steps required to compute the value of a fraction (a flowchart of the same steps is given in Figure 3.3):

> *if |denominator| < 0.0001*
> > *print "Denominator close to zero"*
> *else*
> > *set fraction to numerator/denominator*
> > *print fraction*

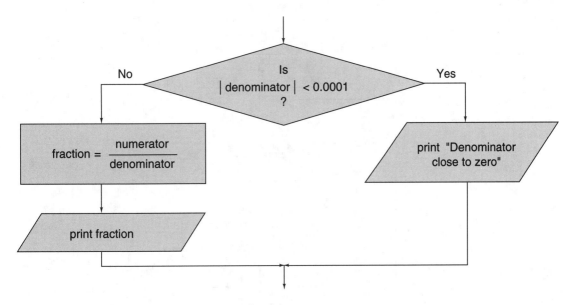

Figure 3.3 *Flowchart for selection structure.*

Note that this structure contains a sequence structure (compute a fraction and then print the fraction) that is executed when the condition is false. We present several variations of the selection structure later in the chapter.

Repetition. The repetition structure allows us to repeat a set of steps as long as a condition is true. For example, we might want to compute a set of velocity values that correspond to time values of 0, 1, 2, . . . , 10 s. In implementing this computation, we certainly do not want to develop a sequential structure that has a statement to compute the velocity for a time of 0, then another statement to compute the velocity for a time of 1, and then another statement to compute the velocity for a time of 2, and so on. This structure would require 11 statements and, if we wanted to compute the velocity values over a longer period of time, could add up to hundreds of statements. If we use the repetition structure instead, we can develop a solution in which we initialize the time to 0. Then, as long as the time value is less than or equal to 10 (or 100 or 1,000 if we wish), we compute and print a velocity value and increment the time value by 1. When the time value is greater than 10 (or 100 or 1,000), we exit the structure. Figure 3.4 contains a flowchart for this repetition structure, and the pseudocode is as follows:

> *set time to 0*
> *while time ≤ 10*
> > *compute velocity*
> > *print velocity*
> > *increment time by 1*

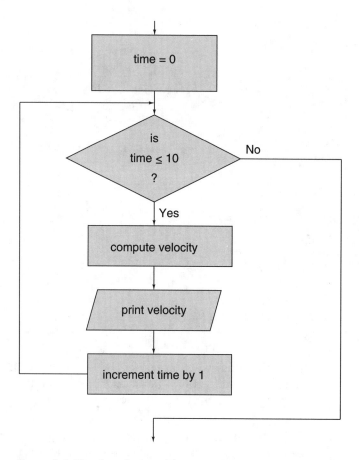

Figure 3.4 *Flowchart for repetition structure.*

In the remaining sections of this chapter, we present the C++ statements for performing selections and repetitions and then develop sample programs that use these structures.

3.2   Conditional Expressions

Because both selection and repetition structures use conditions, we begin with a discussion of them. A condition is an expression that can be evaluated to be true or false, and it is composed of expressions combined with relational and, sometimes, logical operators. In this section, we present both of these types of operators and discuss the order of their evaluation when they are combined in a single condition.

RELATIONAL OPERATORS

The following list gives the **relational operators** that can be used to compare two expressions in C++:

Relational Operator	Interpretation
<	is less than
<=	is less than or equal to
>	is greater than
>=	is greater than or equal to
==	is equal to
!=	is not equal to

Blanks can be used on either side of a relational operator, but not within a two-character operator.

Following are some examples of conditions:

```
a < b
x+y >= 10.5
fabs(denominator) < 0.0001
```

Given the values of the identifiers in these conditions, we can evaluate each condition to be true or false. For example, if **a** is equal to 5 and **b** is equal to 8.4, then **a<b** is a true condition. If **x** is equal to 2.3 and **y** is equal to 4.1, then **x+y >= 10.5** is a false condition. If **denominator** is equal to -0.0025, then **fabs(denominator)** *Style* **< 0.0001** is a false condition. *Note that we use spaces around the relational operator in a logical expression, but not around the arithmetic operators in a condition.*

In C++, a true condition is assigned a value of 1, and a false condition is assigned a value of 0. Therefore, the following statement is valid:

```
d = b>c;
```

If **b>c**, then the value of **d** is 1; otherwise the value of **d** is 0. Because a condition is given a value, it is then valid to use a value in place of the condition. For example, consider the statement

```
if (a)
   count++;
```

If the value of the condition is 0, then the condition is assumed to be false; if the value is not 0, then the condition is assumed to be true. Therefore, in the preceding statement, the value of **count** will be incremented if **a** is not 0.

LOGICAL OPERATORS

Logical operators **Logical operators** compare conditions. C++ supports three logical operators—**not, and,** and **or,** represented by the following symbols:

Logical Operator	Symbol
not	!
and	&&
or	||

For example, consider the condition

```
a<b && b<c
```

The relational operators have higher precedence than the logical operator; therefore, this condition is read "**a** is less than **b**, and **b** is less than **c**." Given values for **a**, **b**, and **c**, we can evaluate the condition as true or false. For example, if **a** is equal to 1, **b** is equal to 5, and **c** is equal to 8, then the condition is true. If **a** is equal to −2, **b** is equal to 9, and **c** is equal to 2, then the condition is false. *Note that, to make a logical statement more readable, we insert spaces around the logical operator, but not around the relational operators.*

Style

If **a** and **b** are conditions, then the logical operators can be used to generate the new conditions **a && b**, **a || b**, **!a**, and **!b**. The condition **a && b** is true only if both **a** and **b** are true. The condition **a || b** is true if either or both of **a** and **b** are true. The **!** operator changes the value of the condition with which it is used. Thus, the condition **!a** is true only if **a** is false, and the condition **!b** is true only if **b** is false. These definitions are summarized in Table 3.1.

When an expression with logical operators is executed, C++ will evaluate only as much of the expression as is necessary to evaluate it. For example, if **a** is false, then the expression **a && b** is also false, and there is no need to evaluate **b**. Similarly, if **a** is true, then the expression **a || b** is true, and there is no need to evaluate **b**.

PRECEDENCE AND ASSOCIATIVITY

A condition can contain several logical operators. For instance, the condition

```
!(b==c || b==5.5)
```

contains the two logical operators **!** and **||**. The hierarchy of logical operators, from highest to lowest, is **!**, **&&**, **||**, but parentheses can be used to change the order of predecence. In the foregoing example, the expressions **b==c** and **b==5.5** are evaluated first. Suppose **b** is equal to 3 and **c** is equal to 5. Then neither expression is true, so the expression **b==c || b==5.5** is false. We then apply the **!** operator to the false condition, which gives a true condition. Blanks cannot be used to separate the characters in either **||** or **&&**. A common error is to use **=** instead of **==** in a logical expression.

A condition can contain both arithmetic operators and relational operators, as well as logical operators. Table 3.2 shows the precedence and the order of associativity for all of these elements.

A	B	A && B	A || B	!A	!B
false	false	false	false	true	true
false	true	false	true	true	false
true	false	false	true	false	true
true	true	true	true	false	false

TABLE 3.1 Logical Operators

TABLE 3.2 Precedence and Associativity for Arithmetic, Relational, and Logical Operators

Precedence	Operation	Associativity
1	( )	innermost first
2	+ - ++ -- cast !	right to left (unary)
3	* / %	left to right
4	+ -	left to right
5	< <= > >=	left to right
6	== !=	left to right
7	&&	left to right
8	||	left to right
9	= += -= *= /= %=	right to left

Practice!

Determine whether the following conditions are true or false. Assume that the following variables have been declared and given the values shown.

a [5.5]   b [1.5]   k [-3]

1. `a < 10+k`   2. `a+b >= 6.5`   3. `!(a == 3*b)`

4. `-k <= k+6`   5. `a<10 && a>5`   6. `fabs(k)>3 || k<b-a`

3.3   Selection Statements

The `if` statement allows us to test a condition and then execute statements based on whether the condition is true or false. C++ contains two forms of the `if` statement: the simple `if` statement and the `if/else` statement.

SIMPLE `if` STATEMENT

The simple `if` statement has the following general form:

```
if (condition)
    statement 1;
```

Style

If the condition is true, we execute statement 1; if the condition is false, we skip statement 1. *The statement within the `if` statement is indented so that it is easier to visualize the structure of the program from its statements.*

Compound statement

If we wish to execute several statements (a sequence structure) if the condition is true, we use a **compound statement**, or **block**, which is composed of a set of statements enclosed in braces. The location of the braces is a matter of style; two common styles are as follows:

Style 1

```
if (condition)
{
    statement 1;
    statement 2;
        .
        .
        .
    statement n;
}
```

Style 2

```
if (condition) {
    statement 1;
    statement 2;
        .
        .
        .
    statement n;
}
```

In the solutions presented in the text, we use the first convention, in which the braces are on lines by themselves. Although this makes the program a little longer, it also makes it easier to notice if a brace has been mistakenly omitted. Figure 3.5 shows flowcharts of the program control with simple `if` statements containing either one statement to execute or several statements to execute if the condition is true.

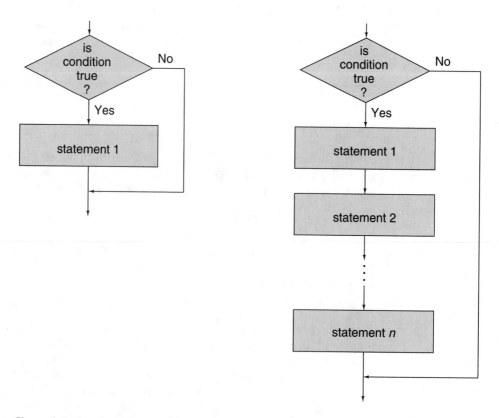

Figure 3.5 *Flowcharts for selection statements.*

A specific example of an **if** statement is

```
if (a < 50)
{
    ++count;
    sum += a;
}
```

If **a** is less than 50, then **count** is incremented by 1 and **a** is added to **sum**; otherwise these two statements are skipped.

If statements can be nested; the following example includes an **if** statement within another **if** statement:

```
if (a < 50)
{
    ++count;
    sum += a;
    if (b > a)
        b = 0;
}
```

Style

If **a** is less than 50, we increment **count** by 1 and add **a** to **sum**. In addition, if **b** is greater than **a**, then we also set **b** to zero. If **a** is not less than 50, then we skip all these statements. *Be sure to indent each nested* **if** *statement.*

if/else STATEMENT

An **if/else** statement allows us to execute one set of statements if a condition is true and a different set if the condition is false. The simplest form of an **if/else** statement is

```
if (condition)
    statement 1;
else
    statement 2;
```

Empty statement

Statements 1 and 2 can be replaced, if desired, by compound statements. Statement 1 or statement 2 can also be an **empty statement**, which is just a semicolon. If statement 2 is an empty statement, then the **if/else** statement should probably be posed as a simple **if** statement. In some situations, it is convenient to use an empty statement for statement 1; however, even these statements can be rewritten as a simple **if** statement with the condition reversed. For example, the following two statements are equivalent:

```
if (a < b)            if (a >= b)
    ;                     count++;
else
    count++;
```

Now consider the `if/else` statement

```
if (d <= 30)
    velocity = 0.425 + 0.00175*d*d;
else
    velocity = 0.625 + 0.12*d - 0.0025*d*d;
```

In this statement, **velocity** is computed with the first assignment statement if the distance **d** is less than or equal to 30; otherwise, **velocity** is computed with the second assignment statement. A flowchart for this `if/else` statement is shown in Figure 3.6.

Another example of the `if/else` statement is

```
if (fabs(denominator) < 0.0001)
    cout << "Denominator close to zero";
else
{
    fraction = numerator/denominator;
    cout << "fraction = " << fraction << endl;
}
```

In this example, we examine the absolute value of the variable **denominator**. If the value is close to zero, we print a message indicating that we cannot perform the division. If the value of **denominator** is not close to zero, we compute and print the value of the fraction. The flowchart for this statement was shown in Figure 3.3.

Next, consider the following set of nested `if/else` statements:

```
if (x > y)
    if (y < z)
        k++;
    else
        m++;
else
    j++;
```

The value of **k** is incremented when **x>y** and **y<z**. The value of **m** is incremented when **x>y** and **y>=z**. The value of **j** is incremented when **x<=y**. With careful indenting, this statement is straightforward to follow. Suppose that we now eliminate the **else** portion of the inner `if` statement. If we keep the same indenting, the entire statement becomes

```
if (x > y)
    if (y < z)
        k++;
else
    j++;
```

It might appear that **j** is still incremented when **x<=y**, but that is not correct. The C++ compiler will associate an **else** statement with the closest **if** statement

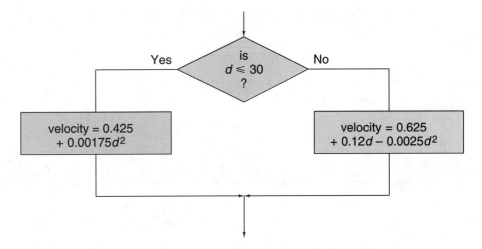

Figure 3.6 *Flowcharts for selection structure.*

within a block. Therefore, no matter what indenting is used, the preceding statement is executed as if it were the statement

```
if (x > y)
    if (y < z)
        k++;
    else
        j++;
```

Thus, **j** is incremented when **x>y** and **y>=z**. If we intended that **j** be incremented
when **x<=y**, then we would need to use braces to define the inner statement as
a block:

```
if (x > y)
{
    if (y < z)
        k++;
}
else
  j++;
```

Style

To avoid confusion and possible errors when using nested **if/else** *statements,
you should routinely use braces to define the blocks of statements that go together.*

In this section, we have presented a number of ways to compare values
in selection statements. A caution is necessary when comparing floating-point
values. For instance, in the example on page 70, we did not compare **denominator**
to zero, but instead used a condition to see whether the absolute value of

denominator was less than a small value. Similarly, if we wanted to know whether **y** was close to the value 10.5, we should use a condition such as

```
fabs(y-10.5) <= 0.0001
```

instead of **y == 10.5**. In general, do not use the equality operator with floating-point values.

Practice!

In the following problems, give the corresponding C++ statements. Assume that the variables have been declared and have reasonable values.

1. If **time** is greater than 15, increment **time** by 1.
2. When the square root of **poly** is less than 0.5, print the value of **poly**.
3. If the difference between **volt_1** and **volt_2** is larger than 10, print the values of **volt_1** and **volt_2**.
4. If the natural logarithm of **x** is greater than or equal to 3, set **time** equal to zero and decrement **count**.
5. If **dist** is less than 50 and **time** is greater than 10, increment **time** by 2; otherwise, increment **time** by 2.5.
6. If **dist** is greater than or equal to 100, increment **time** by 2. If **dist** is between 50 and 100, increment **time** by 1. Otherwise, increment **time** by 0.5.

3.4   Loop Structures

Loops

Loops are used to implement repetitive structures. C++ contains three different loop structures: the **while** loop, the **do/while** loop, and the **for** loop. In addition, C++ allows us to use two additional statements with loops to modify their performance: the **break** statement and the **continue** statement.

Before discussing loop structures, we present two debugging suggestions that are useful when you are trying to find errors in programs that contain loops. In compiling longer programs, it is not uncommon to get a large number of compiler errors. Rather than trying to find each error separately, we suggest that you recompile your program after correcting several obvious syntax errors. One error will often generate several error messages. Some of these messages may describe errors that are not actually in your program, but were printed because the original error confused the compiler.

The second debugging suggestion relates to errors inside a loop. When you want to determine whether the steps in a loop are working the way you intend them to work, include `cout` statements in the loop to provide a memory snapshot of key variables each time the loop is executed. Then, if there is an error, you have much of the information that you need to determine what is causing the error.

`while` LOOP

The general form of a `while` loop is

```
while (condition)
    statement;
```

The condition is evaluated before the statement within the loop is executed. (The statement may be a compound statement.) If the condition is false, the loop statement is skipped, and execution continues with the statement following the `while` loop. If the condition is true, then the loop statement is executed, and the condition is evaluated again. If it is still true, then the statement is executed again, and the condition is evaluated once more. This repetition continues until the condition is false. The statement within the loop must modify variables that are used in the condition; otherwise, the value of the condition will never change, and we will either never execute the statement in the loop or never be able to exit the loop. An **infinite loop** is generated if the condition in a `while` loop is always true. Most systems place a limit on the amount of time that can be used by a program and will generate an execution error when this limit is exceeded. Other systems require that the user enter a special set of characters, such as the control key followed by the character `c` (abbreviated `^c`) to stop or abort the execution of a program. Nearly everyone eventually writes a program that inadvertently contains an infinite loop, so be sure you know the special characters that will abort the execution of a program running on your system.

Infinite loop

The following pseudocode and program use a `while` loop to generate a table for converting degrees to radians. The degree value starts at 0°, is incremented by 10°, and goes through 360°.

Refinement in Pseudocode:
main: set degrees to zero
          while degrees ≤ 360
              convert degrees to radians
              print degrees, radians
              add 10 to degrees

```
//-----------------------------------------------------------
// Program chapter3_1
//
// This program prints a degree-to-radian table
// using a while loop structure.
```

```
#include <iostream.h>
#include <iomanip.h>
#include <stdlib.h>

int main()
{
   //   Define constant and variables.
   const double PI=3.141593;
   int degrees=0;
   double radians;

   //  Print degrees and radians in a loop.
   cout << "Degrees to Radians" << endl;
   while (degrees <= 360)
   {
      radians = degrees*PI/180;
      cout << degrees << "   "
           << setprecision(4) << radians << endl;
      degrees += 10;
   }

   //  Exit program.
   return EXIT_SUCCESS;
}
//-----------------------------------------------------------
```

The first few lines of output from the program are as follows:

```
Degrees to Radians
0    0
10   0.1745
20   0.3491
  .
  .
  .
```

do/while LOOP

The **do/while** loop is similar to the **while** loop, except that the condition is tested at the end of the loop instead of at the beginning. Testing the condition at the end ensures that the **do/while** loop is executed at least once; a **while** loop may not be executed at all if the condition is initially false. The general form of the **do/while** loop is

```
do
   statement;
while (condition);
```

The following pseudocode and program use a **do/while** loop instead of a **while** loop to print the degree-to-radian conversion table printed earlier in Program **chapter3_1**.

Refinement in Pseudocode:

main: set degrees to zero
           do
                     convert degrees to radians
                     print degrees, radians
                     add 10 to degrees
           while degrees ≤ 360

```
//-----------------------------------------------------------
//  Program chapter3_2
//
//  This program prints a degree-to-radian table
//  using a do-while loop structure.

#include <iostream.h>
#include <iomanip.h>
#include <stdlib.h>

int main()
{
   // Define constant and variables.
   const double PI=3.141593;
   int degrees=0;
   double radians;

   // Print degrees and radians in a loop.
   cout << "Degrees to Radians" << endl;
   do
   {
      radians = degrees*PI/180;
      cout << degrees << "   "
           << setprecision(4) << radians << endl;
      degrees += 10;
   } while (degrees <= 360);

   // Exit program.
   return EXIT_SUCCESS;
}
//-----------------------------------------------------------
```

for LOOP

Many programs require loops that are based on the value of a variable that is incremented (or decremented) by the same amount each time through the loop. When the variable reaches a specified value, we want to exit the loop. This type of loop can be implemented as a **while** loop, but it can also be easily implemented with the **for** loop, the general form of which is

```
for (expression_1; expression_2; expression_3)
    statement;
```

Loop-control variable

Expression_1 is used to initialize the **loop-control variable**, **expression_2** specifies the condition that should be true to repeat the loop, and **expression_3** specifies the modification to the loop-control variable.

For example, if we want to execute a loop 10 times, with the value of the variable **k** going from 1 to 10 in increments of 1, we could use either of the following **for** loop structures:

```
for (int k=1; k<11; k++)
    statement;
```

```
for (int k=1; k<=10; k++)
    statement;
```

Note that the integer variable **k** is declared in the **for** statement. Since a variable can be declared anywhere in a C++ program, we should delay declaring **k** until we initialize the **for** loop statement, rather than declaring it at the beginning of the program. This placement emphasizes the relationship of the variable to the loop statement. *In general, a variable should be declared and initialized in the section of code that first uses it.*

Style

If we want to execute a loop with the value of the variable **n** going from 20 to 0 in increments of −2, we could use the loop structure

```
for (int n=20; n>=0; n=n-2)
    statement;
```

This **for** loop could also have been written in the form

```
for (int n=20; n>=0; n-=2)
    statement;
```

Both forms are valid, but the abbreviated form is commonly used because it is shorter.

The following expression computes the number of times that a **for** loop will be executed:

$$\text{floor}\left(\frac{\text{final value} - \text{initial value}}{\text{increment}}\right) + 1$$

If the resulting value is negative, the loop is not executed. Thus, if a **for** statement has the structure

```
for (int k=5; k<=83; k+=4)
    statement;
```

then it would be executed the following number of times:

$$\text{floor}\left(\frac{83 - 5}{4}\right) + 1 = \text{floor}\left(\frac{78}{4}\right) + 1 = 20$$

The value of k would be 5, then 9, then 13, and so on, until k reached the final value of 81. The loop would *not* be executed with the value of 85, because the loop condition is not true when k is equal to 85.

The following pseudocode and program use a **for** loop to print the degree-to-radian conversion table printed earlier with a **while** loop, in Program **chapter3_1**. Note that the pseudocode for the **while** loop and the pseudocode for the **do** loop are identical for this problem.

Refinement in Pseudocode:
main: set degrees to zero
          while degrees ≤ 360
                  convert degrees to radians
                  print degrees, radians
                  add 10 to degrees

```
//------------------------------------------------------------
//  Program chapter3_3
//
//  This program prints a degree-to-radian table
//  using a for loop structure.

#include <iostream.h>
#include <iomanip.h>
#include <stdlib.h>

int main()
{
    //  Define constant and variable.
    const double PI=3.141593;
    double radians;

    //  Print degrees and radians in a loop.
    cout << "Degrees to Radians" << endl;
    for (int degrees=0; degrees<=360; degrees+=10)
    {
        radians = degrees*PI/180;
        cout << degrees << "   "
             << setprecision(4) << radians << endl;
    }

    //  Exit program.
    return EXIT_SUCCESS;
}
//------------------------------------------------------------
```

Observe that the variable **degrees** is declared and initialized in the **for** loop statement, not at the beginning of the program.

Practice!

Determine the number of times that the following **for** loops are executed:

1.  ```
    for (int k=3; k<=20; k++)
        statement;
    ```

2.  ```
    for (k=3; k<=20; ++k)
        statement;
    ```

3.  ```
    for (int count=-2; count<15; count++)
        statement;
    ```

4.  ```
    for (k=-2; k>=-10; k--)
        statement;
    ```

5.  ```
    for (int time=10; time>=0; time--)
        statement;
    ```

6.  ```
    for (time=10; time>=5; time++)
        statement;
    ```

break AND continue STATEMENTS

Iteration

The **break** statement can be used with any of the loop structures presented in this section to exit immediately from the loop in which it is contained. In contrast, the **continue** statement is used to skip the remaining statements in the current pass or **iteration** of the loop and then continue with the next iteration of the loop. Thus, in a **while** loop or a **do/while** loop, the condition is evaluated after the **continue** statement is executed to determine whether the statements in the loop are to be executed again. In a **for** loop, the loop-control variable is modified, and the condition is then evaluated to determine whether the statements in the loop are to be executed again. Both the **break** statement and the **continue** statement are useful in exiting either the current iteration or the entire loop when error conditions are encountered.

To illustrate the difference between the two statements, consider the following loop, which reads values from the keyboard:

```
sum = 0;
for (int k=1; k<21; k++)
{
    cin >> x;
    if (x > 10)
        break;
    sum += x;
}
cout << "sum = " << sum << endl;
```

This loop reads up to 20 values from the keyboard. If all 20 values are less than or equal to 10, then the statements compute the sum of the values and print it. But if a value is read that is greater than 10, then the **break** statement causes control to break out of the loop and execute the **cout** statement. Thus, the sum printed is only the sum of the values up to the value greater than 10.

Now consider this variation of the previous loop:

```
sum = 0;
for (int k=1; k<21; k++)
{
    cin >> x;
    if (x > 10)
        continue;
    sum += x;
}
cout << "sum =  " << sum << endl;
```

Here, the sum of all 20 values is printed if all of the values are less than or equal to 10. However, if a value is greater than 10, then the **continue** statement causes control to skip the rest of the statements in that iteration of the loop and to continue with the next iteration. Hence, the sum printed is the sum of all values in the 20 values that are less than or equal to 10.

3.5   Problem Solving Applied: Weather Balloons

Weather balloons are used to gather temperature and pressure data at various altitudes in the atmosphere. The balloon rises because the density of the helium in it is less than the density of the surrounding air outside of it. As the balloon rises, the surrounding air becomes less dense, and thus, the ascent slows until the balloon reaches a point of equilibrium. During the day, sunlight warms the helium trapped inside the balloon, which causes the helium to expand and become less dense and the balloon to rise higher. During the night, the helium in the balloon cools and becomes more dense, causing the balloon to descend to a lower altitude. The next day, the sun heats the helium again and the balloon rises. Over time, this process generates a set of altitude measurements that can be approximated with a polynomial equation.

Suppose that the following polynomial represents the altitude or height of a weather balloon in meters during the first 48 hours following the launch of the balloon:

$$\text{alt}(t) = -0.12t^4 + 12t^3 - 380t^2 + 4100t + 220$$

The units of t are hours. The corresponding polynomial model for the velocity in meters per hour of the balloon is

$$v(t) = -0.48t^3 + 36t^2 - 760t + 4100$$

Print a table of values of the altitude and the velocity of this weather balloon using units of meters and meters/second. Let the user enter the starting time, the increment in time between lines of the table, and the ending time, where all the time values must be less than 48 hours. In addition to printing the table, print the peak altitude, taken from the table, and the corresponding time.

1.   PROBLEM STATEMENT

Using the polynomials that represent the altitude and velocity of a weather balloon, print a table listing units of meters and meters/second. Also, find and print the maximum altitude (or height) of the balloon, taken from the table, and the corresponding time.

2.   INPUT/OUTPUT DESCRIPTION

The following I/O diagram shows the user input that represents the starting time, time increment, and ending time for generating the table. The output is the table of altitude and velocity values and the maximum altitude and its corresponding time.

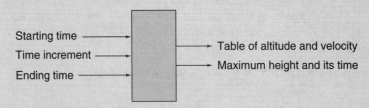

3.   HAND EXAMPLE

Assume that the starting time is 0 hours, the time increment is 1 hour, and the ending time is 5 hours. To obtain the correct units, we need to divide the velocity value in meters/hour by 3,600, yielding meters/second (m/s). Using a calculator, we can then compute the following values:

Time	Altitude (m)	Velocity(m/s)
0	220.00	1.14
1	3,951.88	0.94
2	6,994.08	0.76
3	9,414.28	0.59
4	11,277.28	0.45
5	12,645.00	0.32

We can also determine the maximum altitude from this table: 12,645.00 meters, 5 hours into the flight.

4.   ALGORITHM DEVELOPMENT

We first develop the decomposition outline, because it breaks the solution into a series of sequential steps.

Decomposition Outline:

1.   *Get user input to specify times for the table.*
2.   *Generate and print conversion table, and find maximum height and corresponding time.*
3.   *Print maximum height and corresponding time.*

The second step in the decomposition outline represents a loop in which we generate the table and, at the same time, keep track of the maximum height. As we refine this outline, and particularly step 2, into more detail, we need to think carefully about finding the maximum height. Look back at the hand example. Once the table has been printed, it is easy to look at it and select the maximum height. However, when the computer is computing and printing the table, it does not have all the data at one time; it only has the information for the current line in the table. Therefore, to keep track of the maximum height, we need to specify a separate variable in which to store it. Each time that we compute a new height, we will compare it with the maximum value. If the new value is larger, we replace the maximum with it. We will also need to keep track of the corresponding time. The following refinement in pseudocode outlines these new steps.

Refinement in Pseudocode:

main: *read initial, increment, final values from keyboard*
             set max_height to zero
             set max_time to zero
             print table heading
             set time to initial
             while time<=final
                   compute height and velocity
                   print height and velocity
                   if height>max_height
                         set max_height to height
                         set max_time to time
                   add increment to time
             print max_time and max_height

The steps in the pseudocode are now detailed enough to convert into C++. Note that we convert the velocity from meters/hour to meters/second in the **cout** statement.

```
//----------------------------------------------------------
//  Program chapter3_4
//
//  This program prints a table of height and
//  velocity values for a weather balloon.
```

```cpp
#include <iostream.h>
#include <iomanip.h>
#include <stdlib.h>
#include <math.h>

int main()
{
    // Define variables.
    double initial, increment, final;

    // Get user input.
    cout << "Enter initial value for table (in hours): ";
    cin >> initial;
    cout << "Enter increment between lines (in hours): ";
    cin >> increment;
    cout << "Enter final value for table (in hours): ";
    cin >> final;

    // Print report heading.
    cout << endl
         << "Weather Balloon Information" << endl;
    cout << "Time      Height     Velocity" << endl;
    cout << "(hr)      (m)         (m/s)" << endl;

    // Compute and print report.
    double height, velocity, max_time=0, max_height=0;
    for (double time=initial; time<=final; time+=increment)
    {
        height = -0.12*pow(time,4) + 12*pow(time,3)
                 - 380*time*time + 4100*time + 220;
        velocity = -0.48*pow(time,3) + 36*time*time
                   - 760*time + 4100;
        cout << setw(4) << setprecision(2) << time << "   "
             << setw(8) << setprecision(2) << height << "    "
             << setprecision(2) << velocity/3600 << endl;
        if (height > max_height)
        {
            max_height = height;
            max_time = time;
        }
    }

    // Print maximum height and corresponding time.
    cout << endl << "Maximum balloon height was "
         << setprecision(2) << max_height
         << " m" << endl;
    cout << "and it occurred at " << setprecision(2)
         << max_time << " hr." << endl;

    // Exit program.
    return EXIT_SUCCESS;
}
//-----------------------------------------------------------
```

5. TESTING

If we use the data from the hand example to test Program `chapter3_4`, we obtain the following results:

```
Enter initial value for table (in hours): 0
Enter increment between lines (in hours): 1
Enter final value for table (in hours): 5

Weather Balloon Information
Time      Height     Velocity
(hr)      (m)        (m/s)
   0           220   1.14
   1      3.95e+03   0.94
   2      6.99e+03   0.76
   3      9.41e+03   0.59
   4      1.13e+04   0.45
   5      1.26e+04   0.32

Maximum balloon height was 1.26e+04 m
and it occurred at 5 hr.
```

Figure 3.7 contains plots of the altitude and velocity of the balloon for a period of 48 hours. From the plots, we can see the periods during which the balloon rises or falls.

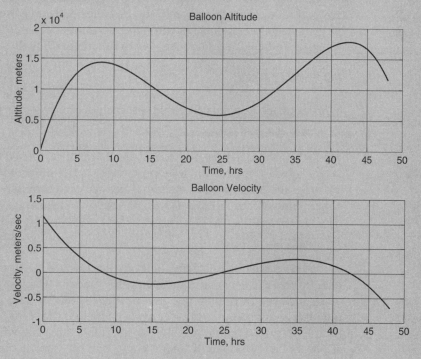

Figure 3.7 *Weather balloon altitude and velocity.*

3.6   Data Files

Solving engineering problems often involves large amounts of data. The data can be generated by the program as output, or the data can be input data that are used by the program. It is not generally feasible either to print large amounts of data to the screen or to read large amounts of data from the keyboard. In these

Data files

cases, we usually use **data files** to store the data. Data files are similar to the program files that we create to store our C++ programs. In fact, a C++ program file is an input data file to the C++ compiler, and the object program is an output file from the C++ compiler. In this section, we discuss the C++ statements used for interacting with data files and give examples that generate data files and that read information from data files.

When debugging programs that read information from data files, echo (i.e., print) the information read from the file to be sure that the data are being read properly. If the data values are all zero or are unusual numbers, it may be that the

program cannot find the file because it is in a directory that the program cannot access. The solution is either to move the file to a directory that the program can access or to change some of the operating system parameters so that the program can find the file.

In the examples that follow, we use files containing data received from a seismometer—a special kind of sensor that detects earth motion. Seismometers are usually buried near the surface of the earth; they are so sensitive that they can record tidal motion as well as earthquakes, even though they may be located hundreds of miles from the ocean. Data are collected from seismometers all over the earth and sent by satellite to central locations for analysis. By studying these data, scientists and engineers may be able to predict earthquakes.

I/O STATEMENTS

In order to access a data file, we must include the preprocessor directive

```
#include <fstream.h>
```

where the header file **fstream.h** contains information related to manipulating a file.

File object

Each data file used in a program needs a **file object** to attach the data file to the program. If a program uses two files, then each should be given a different file object name for readability. We use the following statement to create a file object named **sensor1**:

```
fstream sensor1;
```

After a file object is defined, it can be associated with a specific file using the **open** function. The two arguments for this function are the file name, which needs

File access mode

to be enclosed in double quotes, and the file status (also called the **file access mode**). The access mode tells the system whether the file is an input file or an output file. If we are going to read information from a file with a program, the file access mode is **ios::in**. If we are going to write information to a file with a program, the file access mode is **ios::out**. Thus, the following statement specifies that the file object **sensor1** is going to be used with a file named **sensor1.dat**, from which we will read information:

```
sensor1.open("sensor1.dat", ios::in);
```

The general form of the statements used to create a file object and attach it to a data file are as follows:

```
fstream object_name;
object_name.open("file_name", access mode);
```

These two statements can be combined in the statement

```
fstream object_name("file_name", access mode);
```

 Since some operating systems are not case sensitive, we will use all lowercase letters in file names to avoid any potential problems.

Once an input file and its object have been specified, we can read information from the file much as we would read information from the keyboard. However, instead of using **cin**, we use the file object; the **>>** operator is still cascaded to receive data from the file. If each line in the **sensor1.dat** file contains a time and a sensor reading, we can read one line of this information and store the values in the variables **time** and **motion** with the file input statement

```
sensor1 >> time >> motion;
```

The difference between the file input statement and the **cin** statement is that the first word in the file input statement is the file object name; otherwise, both statements are the same. The **cin** statement converts the characters received from the keyboard to values, and the file input statement converts the characters from the lines in the data file to values.

In a similar manner, if the file is an output file, we can write information to it with the file output statement. The first word of the file output statement is also the file object name, and the rest of the statement is the same as the **cout** statement. The **<<** operator is still used to send data to the file. For example, consider Program **chapter3_4**, which computed and printed a table of time, altitude, and velocity data. If we wanted to modify this program so that it generated a data file containing the same data, we could use an object name **balloon** that would be associated with an output file named **balloon.dat** using the statements

```
fstream balloon;
balloon.open("balloon.dat", ios::out);
```

where the file access mode is **ios::out**. Then, as we compute the information on time, height, and velocity, we can write it to the file with the file output statement

```
balloon << time << height << velocity/3600 << endl;
```

The **endl** reference causes a skip to a new line after each group of three values is written to the file.

The **close** function, used to close a file after we are finished with it, does not have an argument. Its general form is

```
object_name.close()
```

Thus, to close the two files used in the examples we have been considering, we can use the following statements:

```
sensor1.close();
balloon.close();
```

There is no distinction between closing an input file and closing an output file. If a file has not been closed when the **return** statement is executed, it will automatically be closed. It is important to note that executing the **close** function does not destroy our file object; it only closes the data file. The object still exists, and therefore, we could use another **open** function to attach it to a new data file.

READING DATA FILES

In order to read information from a data file, we must first know some details about the file. Obviously, we must know the file name so that we can use the **open** statement to associate the file with its object. We must also know the order and data type of the values stored in the file so that we can declare corresponding identifiers correctly. Finally, if we attempt to execute a file input statement after we have read all the data in the file, an error occurs. Therefore, we need to know how much information is in the file—that is, we have to be able to ascertain when we have read all the data.

Records

Data files generally have one of three common structures. Some files are generated such that the first line in the file will tell us the number of lines (also called **records**) with information that follow. For example, suppose that a file has 150 records containing time and data values received from a sensor. The file could be constructed such that the first line contains only the value 150, and that line would then be followed by 150 lines containing the time and data values. To read the records from this file, we initially read the value from the first line in the file and then use a **for** loop to read the rest of the information. This type of loop is also

Counter-controlled loop

called a **counter-controlled loop**.

Trailer

Another form of file structure uses a **trailer** or **sentinel** signal. These signals are special data values that indicate the last record in a file. For example, the previous data file constructed with a sentinel signal would contain the 150 lines of information followed by a line with special values, such as –999.0 for the time and data value. Sentinel signals must be values that could not appear as regular data, in order to avoid confusion. To read data from this type of file, we use a **while** loop with a condition that is true as long as the value read is not the sentinel signal.

Sentinel-controlled loop

Such a loop is called a **sentinel-controlled loop**.

The third data file structure contains only valid data; it does not contain an initial line with the number of valid data records that follow, and it does not contain a trailer or sentinel signal. For this type of data file, we use the value returned by the **eof** function to help us determine when we have read the last line of the file. To read data from the file, we use a **while** loop with a condition that is true as long as we are not at the end of the file.

We next present some programs for reading data received from a sensor and printing a summary report that contains the number of values read and the average value, the maximum value, and the minimum value. Each of the three common file formats discussed will be used.

Specified Number of Records. Suppose that the first record in the sensor data file contains an integer that specifies the number of records with data that follow. Then the file appears something like the following:

```
sensor1.dat file
10
0.0     132.5
0.1     147.2
0.2     148.3
0.3     157.3
0.4     163.2
0.5     158.2
0.6     169.3
0.7     148.2
0.8     137.6
0.9     135.9
```

The process of first reading the number of data points and then using that number to specify the number of times to read data and accumulate information is easily described with the counter-controlled loop. In the following program, the first actual data value is used to initialize the **max_data** and **min_data** values. If we were to set the **min_data** value initially to zero, and all the sensor values were greater than zero, the program would print the erroneous value of zero for the minimum sensor reading.

```
//-----------------------------------------------------------
//   Program chapter3_5
//
//   This program generates a summary report from
//   a data file that has the number of data points
//   in the first record.

#include <iostream.h>
#include <fstream.h>
#include <stdlib.h>

int main()
{
    //  Open file and read the number of data points.
    int num_data_pts;
    fstream sensor1;
    sensor1.open("sensor1.dat", ios::in);
    sensor1 >> num_data_pts;
```

```
//   Read data and compute summary information.
double time, motion, max, min, sum;
sensor1 >> time >> motion;
max = min = sum = motion;
for (int k=2; k<=num_data_pts; k++)
{
    sensor1 >> time >> motion;
    sum += motion;
    if (motion > max)
       max = motion;
    if (motion < min)
       min = motion;
}

//   Print summary information.
cout << "Number of readings:   "
        << num_data_pts << endl;
cout << "Average reading:   "
        << sum/num_data_pts << endl;
cout << "Maximum reading:   " << max << endl;
cout << "Minimum reading:   " << min << endl;

//   Close file and exit program.
sensor1.close();
return EXIT_SUCCESS;
}
//-----------------------------------------------------------
```

Following is the report printed by this program:

```
Number of readings:   10
Average reading:   149.77
Maximum reading:   169.3
Minimum reading:   132.5
```

Trailer or Sentinel Signals. Suppose that the data file **sensor2.dat** contains the same information as **sensor1.dat**, but instead of the number of valid data records appearing at the beginning of the file, a final record contains a trailer signal. The time value on the last line in the file will be negative, indicating that the line does not contain valid information. Note that a second number must be included on the trailer line, since the statement that reads each line expects two values; otherwise, an error would occur. The contents of the data file are as follows:

```
sensor2.dat file
0.0      132.5
0.1      147.2
0.2      148.3
0.3      157.3
0.4      163.2
0.5      158.2
```

```
0.6      169.3
0.7      148.2
0.8      137.6
0.9      135.9
-99      -99
```

The process of reading and accumulating information until we read the trailer signal is easily described using a **while** loop structure, as shown in the following program:

```cpp
//-------------------------------------------------------------
//  Program chapter3_6
//
//  This program generates a summary report from
//  a data file that has a trailer record with
//  negative values.

#include <iostream.h>
#include <fstream.h>
#include <stdlib.h>

int main()
{
   //  Open file and read the first set of data.
   double time, motion;
   fstream sensor2;
   sensor2.open("sensor2.dat", ios::in);
   sensor2 >> time >> motion;

   //  Define and initialize variables.
   int num_data_pts=0;
   double max=motion, min=motion, sum=0;

   //  Update summary data until trailer record read.
   while (time >= 0)
   {
      sum += motion;
      if (motion > max)
         max = motion;
      if (motion < min)
         min = motion;
      num_data_pts++;
      sensor2 >> time >> motion;
   }

   //  Print summary information.
   cout << "Number of readings:   "
        << num_data_pts << endl;
   cout << "Average reading:   "
        << sum/num_data_pts << endl;
   cout << "Maximum reading:   " << max << endl;
   cout << "Minimum reading:   " << min << endl;
```

```
    //  Close file and exit program.
    sensor2.close();
    return EXIT_SUCCESS;
}
//------------------------------------------------------------
```

The report printed by this program using the **sensor2.dat** file is exactly the same as the report printed by the previous program using the **sensor1.dat** file.

eof function

End-of-File Indicator. A special end-of-file indicator is inserted at the end of every data file; the **eof** function (accessed through the **iostream** header file) can be used to detect when this indicator has been reached in reading a data file. Thus, if we want to read information until we run out of data, we can use the **eof** function in the condition for a **while** loop to allow us to continue reading and processing information as long as we are not at the end of the file.

Let us assume that the data file **sensor3.dat** contains the same information as the file **sensor2.dat**, except that it does not include the trailer signal. Then the contents of **sensor3.dat** are as follows:

```
sensor3.dat file
0.0     132.5
0.1     147.2
0.2     148.3
0.3     157.3
0.4     163.2
0.5     158.2
0.6     169.3
0.7     148.2
0.8     137.6
0.9     135.9
```

In the following program, we read and accumulate information until we reach the end of the data file.

```
//------------------------------------------------------------
//   Program chapter3_7
//
//   This program generates a summary report from a data
//   file that contains only data.  The file does not
//   contain initial information or trailer information.

#include <iostream.h>
#include <fstream.h>
#include <stdlib.h>

int main()
{
    //  Open file and read the first set of data.
    double time, motion;
    fstream sensor3;
    sensor3.open("sensor3.dat", ios::in);
    sensor3 >> time >> motion;
```

```
    //  Define and initialize variables.
    int num_data_pts=0;
    double max=motion, min=motion, sum=0;

    //  While not at the end of the file,
    //  read and accumulate information.
    while (!sensor3.eof())
    {
       sum += motion;
       if (motion > max)
          max = motion;
       if (motion < min)
          min = motion;
       num_data_pts++;
       sensor3 >> time >> motion;
    }

    //  Print summary information.
    cout << "Number of readings:  "
         << num_data_pts << endl;
    cout << "Average reading:  "
         << sum/num_data_pts << endl;
    cout << "Maximum reading:  " << max << endl;
    cout << "Minimum reading:  " << min << endl;

    //  Close file and exit program.
    sensor3.close();
    return EXIT_SUCCESS;
}
//-------------------------------------------------------------
```

fail function

The programs in this section work properly if the data files exist and contain the expected information. A division-by-zero error will occur if the number of points is zero. If the program attempts to open a file that does not exist, or that cannot be found because the system is looking on the wrong disk drive, an error will also occur. The **fail function** (also accessed through the **iostream** header file) can be used to determine the success or failure of an open operation; the function returns a true value if the operation failed and a false value if it was successful. In the former case, an appropriate error message can be printed before ending the program. To illustrate the use of this function, we present a modification of the previous program that now uses the **fail** function to determine whether the file has been found.

```
//-------------------------------------------------------------
//  Program chapter3_7_mod
//
//  This program generates a summary report from a data
//  file that contains only data.  The file does not
//  contain initial information or trailer information.
//  If the file is not found, a message is printed.

#include <iostream.h>
#include <fstream.h>
#include <stdlib.h>
```

```
int main()
{
   //  Open file and read the first set of data.
   double time, motion;
   fstream sensor3;
   sensor3.open("sensor3.dat", ios::in);

   //  Check to be sure the file is found.
   if (sensor3.fail())
   {
      cout << "error in opening sensor3.dat" << endl;
      return EXIT_FAILURE;
   }
   else
   {
      //  Read first set of values.
      sensor3 >> time >> motion;

      //  Define and initialize variables.
      int num_data_pts=0;
      double max=motion, min=motion, sum=0;

      (same statements as in Program chapter 3_7 to read
      and accumulate information and to print summary
      information)

      //  Close file and exit program.
      sensor3.close();
      return EXIT_SUCCESS;
   }
}
//------------------------------------------------------------
```

Since the three file structures discussed here are commonly used in engineering and scientific applications, it is important to know which format you are dealing with when you work with a data file. If you make the wrong assumption, you may get incorrect answers instead of an error message. Sometimes the only way to be sure of the file structure is to print the first few lines and the last few lines of the file.

GENERATING A DATA FILE

Generating a data file is very similar to printing a report; instead of writing each line to the screen, however, we write it to a data file. Before we generate the data file, though, we must decide what file structure we want to use. In the previous discussion, we presented the three most common file structures: files with an initial record giving the number of valid records that follow, files with a trailer or sentinel record to indicate the end of the valid data, and files with only valid data records and no special beginning or ending records.

There are advantages and disadvantages to each of the three structures. A file with a trailer signal is simple to use, but choosing a value for the trailer signal must be done carefully so that it does not contain values which could occur in the valid data. If the first record in the data file will contain the number of lines of actual data, we must know how many lines of data will be in the file before we begin to generate it. But this number may not always be easy to determine before executing the program that generates the file. The simplest file to generate is the one that contains only the valid information, with no special information at the beginning or end of the file. If the information in the file is going to be used with a plotting package, it is usually best to use this third file structure, which includes only valid information.

The following program is a modification of Program **chapter3_4**, which printed a table of time, altitude, and velocity values for a weather balloon. In addition to generating a table of information that is displayed on the screen, we write the information to a data file.

```cpp
//------------------------------------------------------------
//   Program chapter3_8
//
//   This program generates a file of height and
//   velocity values for a weather balloon. The
//   information is also printed in a report.

#include <iostream.h>
#include <iomanip.h>
#include <fstream.h>
#include <stdlib.h>
#include <math.h>

int main()
{
   //   Define variables.
   double initial, increment, final;

   //   Get user input.
   cout << "Enter initial value for table (in hours): ";
   cin >> initial;
   cout << "Enter increment between lines (in hours): ";
   cin >> increment;
   cout << "Enter final value for table (in hours): ";
   cin >> final;

   //   Print report heading.
   cout << endl
        << "Weather Balloon Information" << endl;
   cout << "Time      Height     Velocity" << endl;
   cout << "(hr)      (m)         (m/s)" << endl;

   //   Open output file.
   fstream balloon;
   balloon.open("balloon.dat", ios::out);
```

```
//   Compute and print report
//   and write data to a file.
double height, velocity, max_time=0, max_height=0;
for (double time=initial; time<=final; time+=increment)
{
   height = -0.12*pow(time,4) + 12*pow(time,3)
          - 380*time*time + 4100*time + 220;
   velocity = -0.48*pow(time,3) + 36*time*time
            - 760*time + 4100;
   cout << setw(4) << setprecision(2) << time << "   "
        << setw(8) << setprecision(2) << height << "   "
        << setprecision(2) << velocity/3600 << endl;
   balloon << time << "  " << height << "  "
           << velocity/3600 << endl;
   if (height > max_height)
   {
      max_height = height;
      max_time = time;
   }
}

//   Print maximum height and corresponding time.
cout << endl << "Maximum balloon height was "
     << setprecision(2) << max_height
     << " m" << endl;
cout << "and it occurred at " << setprecision(2)
     << max_time << " hr." << endl;

//   Close file and exit program.
balloon.close();
return EXIT_SUCCESS;
}
//------------------------------------------------------------
```

The first few lines of a data file generated by this program using an initial time of 0 hr, an increment of 0.5 hr, and a final time of 48 hr are as follows:

```
0   220   1.138889
0.5   2176.4925   1.035817
1   3951.88   0.937644
1.5   5554.8925   0.844272
        .
        .
        .
```

A plot of the data from this file was shown in Figure 3.7.

CHAPTER SUMMARY

In this chapter, we covered the use of conditions and **if** statements to select other statements to be executed. We also presented techniques for repeating sets of statements that used loops, which can be implemented as **while** loops or **for** loops. These selection and repetition structures are used in most programs. In addition, we included the statements necessary to read information from a data file so that we could use the information in a program. We also presented the statements to generate a data file from a program. Data files are commonly used in solving engineering problems; therefore, they will appear later in many of the solutions we present.

KEY TERMS

block

compound statement

condition

data file

decomposition outline

divide and conquer

empty statement

file access mode

file object

flowchart

for loop

infinite loop

iteration

logical operator

loop

loop-control variable

pseudocode

record

relational operator

repetition

selection

sequence

sentinel signal

stepwise refinement

top-down design

trailer signal

C++ STATEMENT SUMMARY

Declaration for file object:

```
fstream sensor1;
```

if statement:

```
if (temp > 100)
    cout << "Temperature exceeds limit" << endl;
```

if/else statement:

```
if (d <= 30)
    velocity = 4.25 + 0.00175*d*d;
else
    velocity = 0.65 + 0.12*d - 0.0025*d*d;
```

while loop:

```
while (degrees <= 360)
{
   radians = degrees*PI/180;
   cout << degrees << " " << radians << endl;
   degrees += 10;
}
```

do/while loop:

```
do
{
   radians = degrees*PI/180;
   cout << degrees << " " << radians << endl;
   degrees += 10;
} while (degrees <= 360);
```

for loop:

```
for (int degrees=0; degrees<=360; degrees+=10)
{
   radians = degrees*PI/180;
   cout << degrees << " " << radians << endl;
}
```

break statement:

```
break;
```

continue statement:

```
continue;
```

File open statements:

```
sensor1.open("sensor1.dat", ios::in);
balloon.open("balloon.dat", ios::out);
```

File input statement:

```
sensor1 >> time >> motion;
```

File output statement:

```
balloon << time << height << velocity/3600 << endl;
```

File close statement:

```
sensor1.close();
```

Style Notes

1.   Use spaces around the relational operator in a logical expression in a simple condition; use spaces around logical operators, and not around relational operators, in a compound condition.

2. Indent the statements within an **if** statement or inside a loop. If loops or conditional statements are nested, indent each nested set of statements from the previous statements.

3. Use braces within nested **if** statements to identify blocks of statements that are to be executed as a group.

4. Declare and initialize a loop index in its **for** loop statement, instead of at the beginning of the program.

5. Delay declaring and initializing variables until you need them in the program.

DEBUGGING NOTES

1. Be sure to use the relational operator **==** instead of **=** in a condition.

2. Put the braces surrounding a block of statements on lines by themselves; this will help you avoid omitting one of them.

3. Do not use the equality operator with floating-point values; instead, test for values "close to" a desired value.

4. Recompile your program frequently when correcting syntax errors; correcting one error may remove many error messages.

5. Use the **cout** statement to give memory snapshots of the values of key variables when debugging loops.

6. It is easier than you think to generate an infinite loop; be sure you know the special characters needed to abort the execution of a program on your system if the program goes into an infinite loop.

7. When debugging a program that reads a data file, print the values as soon as they are read to check for errors in reading the information.

8. When debugging a program that reads a data file, be sure that the program can access the directory that contains the data file.

9. To avoid problems with operating systems that are not case sensitive, use file names with lowercase letters.

PROBLEMS

Unit Conversions. In each of the following problems, you are asked to generate a table of unit conversions. Include a table heading and column headings. Choose the number of decimal places based on the values to be printed.

1. Generate a table of conversions from degrees to radians. The first line should contain the values for 0°, and the last line should contain the values for 360°. Allow the user to enter the increment to use between lines in the table.

2. Generate a table of conversions from miles per hour (mi/hr) to feet per second (ft/s). Start the mi/hr column at 0, and increment by 5 mi/hr. The last line should contain the value 65 mi/hr. (Recall that 1 mi = 5,280 ft.)

Currency Conversions. In each of the following problems, you are asked to generate a table of currency conversions. Use title and column headings. Assume the following conversion rates:

1 dollar (\$) = 5.045 francs (Fr)

1 yen (Y) = \$ .010239

1 dollar (\$) = 1.4682 deutsche mark (DM)

3. Generate a table of conversions from francs to dollars. Start the francs column at 5 Fr, and increment by 5 Fr. Print 25 lines in the table.

4. Generate a table of conversions from yen to deutsche marks. Start the yen column at 100 Y, and print 25 lines, with the final line containing the value 10,000 Y.

Temperature Conversions. In each of the following problems, you are asked to generate a temperature conversion table. Use the following equations, which give relationships among temperatures in degrees Fahrenheit (T_F), degrees Celsius (T_C), degrees Kelvin (T_K), and degrees Rankine (T_R):

$$T_F = T_R - 459.67$$

$$T_F = \left(\frac{9}{5}\right) T_C + 32$$

$$T_R = \left(\frac{9}{5}\right) T_K$$

5. Write a program to generate a table of conversions from Fahrenheit to Kelvin for values from 0° F to 200° F. Allow the user to enter the increment in degrees F between lines.

6. Write a program to generate a table of conversions from Celsius to Rankine. Allow the user to enter the starting temperature and increment between lines. Print 25 lines in the table.

Suture Packaging. Sutures are strands or fibers used to sew living tissue together after an injury or an operation. Packages of sutures must be sealed carefully before they are shipped to hospitals so that contaminants cannot enter the packages. The object that seals the package is referred to as a sealing die. Generally, sealing dies are heated with an electric heater. For the sealing process to be a success, the sealing die is maintained at an established temperature and must contact the package with a predetermined pressure for an established period. The period in which the sealing die contacts the package is called the dwell time. Assume that the range of parameters for an acceptable seal is as follows:

Temperature: 150–170° C

Pressure: 60–70 psi

Dwell Time: 2–2.5 s

7. A data file named **suture.dat** contains information on batches of sutures that have been rejected during a one-week period. Each line in the file

contains the batch number, the temperature, the pressure, and the dwell time for a rejected batch. The quality control engineer would like to analyze this information and needs a report that computes the percentage of batches rejected due to temperature, the percentage rejected due to pressure, and the percentage rejected due to dwell time. It is possible that a specific batch was rejected for more than one reason and should be counted in all applicable totals. Write a program to compute and print the three percentages. Use the following test data:

Batch Number	Temperature	Pressure	Dwell Time
24551	145.5	62.3	2.23
24582	153.7	63.2	2.52
26553	160.3	58.9	2.51
26623	159.5	58.9	2.01
26642	160.3	61.2	1.98

8. Write a program to read the data file **suture.dat** and make sure that the information relates only to batches that should have been rejected. If any batch should not be in the data file, print a message with appropriate information. Test your program with the data file from Problem 7; then insert records with information about batches that should not have been rejected to make sure that the program will identify these records.

Timber Regrowth. A problem in timber management is to determine how much of an area to leave uncut so that the harvested portion is reforested within a certain period. It is assumed that reforestation takes place at a known rate per year, depending on climate and soil conditions. A reforestation equation expresses this growth as a function of the amount of timber standing and the reforestation rate. For example, if 100 acres are left standing after harvesting, and the reforestation rate is 0.05, then $100 + 0.05 \times 100$, or 105 acres, are forested at the end of the first year. At the end of the second year, the number of acres forested is $105 + 0.05 \times 105$, or 110.25 acres.

9. Assume that there are 14,000 acres with 2,500 acres uncut and that the reforestation rate is 0.02. Print a table showing the number of acres reforested at the end of each year, for a total of 20 years.

10. Modify the program developed in Problem 9 so that the user can enter a number of acres, and the program will determine how many years are required for that number of acres to be completely forested.

4

Courtesy of Alaska Division of Tourism.

GRAND CHALLENGE:
Enhanced Oil and Gas Recovery

The design and construction of the Alaskan pipeline presented numerous engineering challenges. One of the important problems that had to be addressed was protecting the permafrost (the permanently frozen subsoil in arctic or subarctic regions) from the heat of the pipeline itself. The oil flowing in the pipeline is warmed by pumping stations and by friction from the walls of the pipe, so the supports holding the pipeline must be insulated or even cooled to keep them from melting the permafrost at their bases. In addition, the components of the pipeline had to be very reliable because of the inaccessibility of some locations. More importantly, component failure could cause damage to human life, animal life, and the environment around the pipeline.

Modular Programming with Functions

OBJECTIVES

In this chapter, we discuss the importance of dividing programs into functions (or modules) that perform specific operations. In C++, modules are available from libraries such as the Standard C++ library; programmer-defined modules may also be written specifically to accompany a `main` function. This chapter presents several examples of programmer-written functions.

4.1   Modularity

Modules

The execution of a C++ program begins with the statements in the **main** function. A program may also contain other functions, and it may refer to functions in another file or in a library. These functions, or **modules**, are sets of statements that typically perform an operation or that compute a value. For example, the **setw** function sets the field width of a value, and the **sqrt** function computes the square root of a value.

Style

To maintain simplicity and readability in longer and more complex solutions to problems, we develop programs that use a **main** function plus additional functions, instead of using one long **main** function. *By separating a solution into a group of modules, we make each module simpler and easier to understand, thus adhering to the basic guidelines of structured programming presented in Chapter 3.*

The process of developing a solution to a problem is often one of "divide and conquer," as stated when we first discussed the decomposition outline. Since the decomposition outline is a set of sequentially executed steps that solves the problem, it provides a good starting point for selecting potential functions. In fact, it is not uncommon for each step in the decomposition outline to correspond to one or more function references in the **main** function.

Breaking a solution into a set of modules has many advantages. Since a module has a specific purpose, it can be written and tested separately from the rest of the solution. An individual module is smaller than the complete solution, so testing it is easier. And, once a module has been carefully tested, it can be used in new solutions without being retested. For example, suppose that a module is developed to find the average of a group of values. Once this module is written and tested, it can be used in other programs that need to compute an average. This **reusability** is a very important issue in the development of large software systems because it can save development time. In fact, libraries of commonly used modules (such as the Standard C++ library) are often available on computer systems.

Reusability

The use of modules (called **modularity**) frequently reduces the overall length of a program because many solutions include steps that are repeated several places in the program. By incorporating these repetitive steps into a function, we can reference the steps with a single statement each time that they are needed.

Several programmers can work on the same project if it is separated into modules, because the individual modules can be developed and tested independently of each other. This allows the development schedule to be accelerated, as some of the work can then be done in parallel.

Abstraction

The use of modules that have been written to accomplish specific tasks supports the concept of **abstraction**. The modules contain the details of the tasks, and the programmer can reference the modules without worrying about these details. The I/O diagrams that we use in developing a solution to a problem are an example of abstraction: We specify the input information and the output information, without giving the details of how the output information is determined. In a similar way, we can think of modules as "black boxes" that have a specified input and that compute specified information; we can use these modules to help develop a solution. Thus, we are able to operate at a higher level of abstraction to solve problems. For example, the Standard C++ library contains functions that compute the logarithms of values. We can reference these functions without being concerned about their specific details, such as whether the functions are using infinite series approximations or lookup tables to compute the desired logarithms. By using abstraction, we can reduce the development time of software at the same time that we increase its quality.

To summarize, some of the advantages of using modules in solving a problem are the following:

- A module can be written and tested separately from other parts of the solution; thus, module development can be done in parallel for large projects.
- A module is a small part of the solution; thus, testing it separately is easier.
- Once a module is tested carefully, it does not need to be retested before it can be used in solving new problems.
- The use of modules usually reduces the length of a program, making it more readable.
- The use of modules promotes the concept of abstraction, which allows the programmer to "hide" details in modules; this in turn allows us to use modules in a functional sense without being concerned about specific details.

Additional benefits of modules will be pointed out throughout this chapter.

As we begin to develop solutions to more complicated problems, our programs become longer. Therefore, we mention three suggestions for debugging longer programs. First, it is sometimes helpful to run a program using another compiler, since different compilers have different error messages; in fact, some compilers have extensive error messages, while others give very little information about some types of error. Another useful step in debugging a long program is to add comment indicators (//) to some sections of the code so that you can focus on other parts of the program. Of course, you must be careful that you do not comment out statements that affect variables needed for the parts of the program that you want to test. Finally, test complicated functions by themselves. This is usually done with a special program called a **driver**, whose purpose is to provide a simple interface between you and the function that you are testing. Typically, the driver asks you to enter the parameters that you want passed to the function, and it then prints the value returned by the function.

4.2   Programmer-Defined Functions

Invoked

As mentioned at the beginning of the previous section, the execution of a program always begins with the **main** function. Additional functions are called, or **invoked**, when the program encounters function names. These additional functions must be defined in the file containing the **main** function or in another available file or library of files. (If the function is included in a system library file, as is the **sqrt** function, it is often called a **library function**; other functions are usually

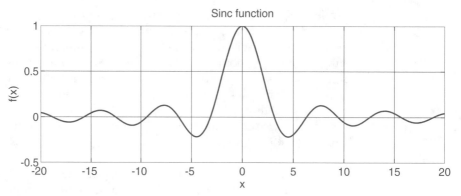

Figure 4.1 *Sinc function in [−20,20].*

called programmer-written or **programmer-defined functions**.) After executing the statements in a function, the program continues with the statement following the function reference.

FUNCTION DEFINITION

The sinc(x) function, plotted in Figure 4.1, is commonly used in many engineering applications. The most common definition of sinc(x) is

$$f(x) = \frac{\sin(x)}{x}$$

(The sinc(x) function is also occasionally defined to be $[\sin(\pi x)]/(\pi x)$.) The values of this function can be easily computed, except for sinc(0), which gives an indeterminate form of 0/0. In this case, L'Hôpital's theorem from calculus can be used to prove that sinc(0) = 1.

Suppose we want to develop a program that allows the user to enter interval limits **a** and **b**. The program is to compute and print 21 values of sinc(x) for values of **x** evenly spaced between **a** and **b**, inclusively. Thus, the first value of **x** should be **a**. An increment should then be added to obtain the next value of **x**, and so on, until the 21st value, which should be **b**. Therefore, the increment in **x** is

$$x\_increment = \frac{interval\ width}{20}$$
$$= \frac{b - a}{20}$$

Select values for **a** and **b**, and convince yourself that, with this increment, and with **a** as the first value, the 21st value will be **b**.

Since sinc(x) is not part of the mathematical functions provided by the Standard C++ library, we implement it in two ways. In one solution, we include the statements that perform the computations of sinc(x) in the **main** function; in the other solution, we write a programmer-defined function to compute sinc(x) and then reference the function each time that the computations are needed. We present both solutions now, so that you can compare them.

Solution 1:

```
//-----------------------------------------------------------
//   Program chapter4_1
//
//   This program prints 21 values of the sinc
//   function in the interval [a,b] using
//   computations within the main function.

#include <iostream.h>
#include <iomanip.h>
#include <stdlib.h>
#include <math.h>

int main()
{
    //   Define variables.
    double a, b, new_x, sinc_x;

    //   Get interval endpoints from the user.
    cout << "Enter endpoints a and b (a<b): " << endl;
    cin >> a >> b;
    double x_incr = (b - a)/20;

    //   Compute and print table of sinc(x) values.
    cout << "x and sinc(x) " << endl;
    for (int k=0; k<=20; k++)
    {
        new_x = a + k*x_incr;
        if (fabs(new_x) < 0.0001)
            sinc_x = 1.0;
        else
            sinc_x = sin(new_x)/new_x;
        cout << setw(4) << new_x << "   "
             << setprecision(4) << sinc_x << endl;
    }

    //   Exit program.
    return EXIT_SUCCESS;
}
//-----------------------------------------------------------
```

Solution 2:

```
//-----------------------------------------------------------
//   Program chapter4_2
//
//   This program prints 21 values of the sinc
//   function in the interval [a,b] using a
//   programmer-defined function.
```

```cpp
#include <iostream.h>
#include <iomanip.h>
#include <stdlib.h>
#include <math.h>

int main()
{
   //  Define variables and function prototype.
   double a, b, new_x;
   double sinc(double x);

   //  Get interval endpoints from the user.
   cout << "Enter endpoints a and b (a<b): " << endl;
   cin >> a >> b;
   double x_incr = (b - a)/20;

   //  Compute and print table of sinc(x) values.
   cout << "x and sinc(x) " << endl;
   for (int k=0; k<=20; k++)
   {
      new_x = a + k*x_incr;
      cout << setw(4) << new_x << "  "
           << setprecision(4) << sinc(new_x) << endl;
   }

   //  Exit program.
   return EXIT_SUCCESS;
}
//-----------------------------------------------------------
//  This function evaluates the sinc function.
//
double sinc(double x)
{
   if (fabs(x) < 0.0001)
      return 1.0;
   else
      return sin(x)/x;
}
//-----------------------------------------------------------
```

The following output represents an interaction that could occur with either program:

```
Enter endpoints a and b (a<b):
-5 5
x and sinc(x)
  -5  -0.1918
-4.5  -0.2172
  -4  -0.1892
-3.5  -0.1002
  -3   0.047
-2.5   0.2394
  -2   0.4546
```

-1.5	0.665
-1	0.8415
-0.5	0.9589
0	1
0.5	0.9589
1	0.8415
1.5	0.665
2	0.4546
2.5	0.2394
3	0.047
3.5	-0.1002
4	-0.1892
4.5	-0.2172
5	-0.1918

Figure 4.2 contains plots of the 21 values computed for four different intervals [a,b]. Since the program computes only 21 values, the resolution in the plots is affected by the size of the interval; a smaller interval has better resolution than a larger interval. Now that you have seen an example of a program with a programmer-defined function, we present a more general discussion of the statements in a function.

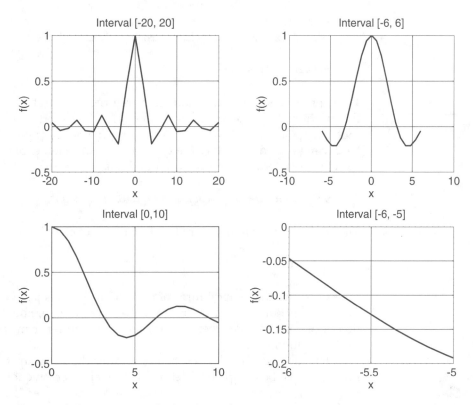

Figure 4.2 *Program output for four intervals.*

A function consists of a definition statement followed by the function body. The first part of the definition statement defines the type of value that is returned by the function (the return_type); if the function does not return a value, the type is **void**. The function name and parameter list follow the return_type. Thus, the general form of a function is

```
return_type function_name(parameter declarations)
{
    function body
}
```

The parameter declarations represent the information passed to the function; if there are no input parameters (also called arguments), then the parameter declarations should be **void**. Additional variables used by a function are defined in the declarations of the function body. The declarations and the statements within a function are enclosed in braces; they constitute the body of the function. *The function name should be selected to help document the purpose of the function. Comments should also be included within the function to further describe the purpose of the function and to document the steps. We also use a comment line with dashes to separate a programmer-defined function from the* **main** *function and from other programmer-defined functions.*

All functions should include a **return** statement, which has the general form

```
return expression;
```

The expression specifies the value to be returned to the statement that referenced the function. The expression type should match the return_type indicated in the function definition to avoid potential errors. The cast operator (discussed in Chapter 2) can be used to specify the type of the expression explicitly if necessary. A **void** function does not return a value and thus has the general definition statement

```
void function_name(parameter declarations)
```

The **return** statement in a **void** function does not contain an expression:

```
return;
```

Compare the general form of a function that has just been described with the **sinc** function defined in Program **chapter4_2**. Also, note that the **main** function of the program is easier to read, since it is shorter than the **main** function in the first solution.

Functions can be defined before or after the **main** function. However, one function must be completely defined before another function definition begins; function definitions cannot be nested within each other. *In our programs, we include the* **main** *function first, and then additional functions are included in the order in which they are referenced in the program.*

We now look more closely at the interaction between a statement that references a function and the function itself.

FUNCTION PROTOTYPE

The **main** function presented in Program **chapter4_2** contains the following statement in its declarations:

```
double sinc(double x);
```

Function prototype

This statement is a **function prototype** statement, or function declaration. It informs the compiler that the **main** function will reference a function named **sinc**, that the **sinc** function expects a **double** parameter, and that the **sinc** function returns a **double** value. The identifier **x** is not being defined as a variable; it is just used to indicate that a value is expected as an argument by the sinc function. In fact, it is valid to include only the argument types in the function prototype statement:

```
double sinc(double);
```

Style

Both prototype statements give the same information to the compiler. *We recommend using parameter identifiers in prototype statements because the identifiers help document the order and definition of the parameters.*

A function prototype can be included with the preprocessor directives; or, because a function prototype is defining the type of value being returned by the function, it can also be included with other variable declarations. For example, the definitions of Program **chapter4_2** are:

```
//  Define variables and function prototype.
double a, b, new_x;
double sinc(double x);
```

These statements could also have been written in the following form:

```
//  Define variables and function prototype.
double a, b, new_x, sinc(double x);
```

Style

In our programs, we list function prototypes on separate declaration statements to make it easier to identify them.

Function prototype statements should be included for all functions referenced in a program. Header files, such as **iostream.h** and **math.h**, contain the prototype statements for many of the functions in the Standard C++ library; otherwise we would need to include individual prototype statements for functions such as **setw** and **sqrt** in our programs. If a programmer-defined function references other programmer-defined functions, then it will also need additional prototype statements.

If a program references a large number of programmer-defined functions, it becomes cumbersome to include all of the associated function prototype statements. In these cases, a custom header file can be defined that contains the function prototypes. A header file must have a file name that ends with the suffix **.h**. The file is then referenced with an **include** statement, using double quotes around the file name. Custom header files are often used to accompany routines that are shared by programmers.

PARAMETER LIST

Formal
parameters

Actual
parameters

The definition statement of a function defines the parameters that are required by the function; these are called **formal parameters**. Any statement that references the function must include values that correspond to the parameters; these are called **actual parameters**. For example, consider the **sinc** function developed earlier in this section. The definition statement of this function is

```
double sinc(double x)
```

and the statement from the **main** program that references the function is

```
cout << new_x << "   " << sinc(new_x);
```

Thus, the variable **x** is the formal parameter and the variable **new_x** is the actual parameter. When the reference to the **sinc** function in the **cout** statement is executed, the value in the actual parameter is copied to the formal parameter, and the steps in the **sinc** function are executed using the new value in **x**. The value returned by the **sinc** function is then printed. It is important to note that the value in the formal parameter is not moved back to the actual parameter when the function completes execution. We illustrate these steps with a memory snapshot that shows the transfer of the value from the actual parameter to the formal parameter, assuming that the value of **new_x** is 5.0:

Actual Parameter   **Formal Parameter**

new_x | 5.0 | →   x | 5.0 |

After the value in the actual parameter is copied to the formal parameter, the steps in the **sinc** function are executed. When you are debugging a function, it is a good idea to use **cout** statements to provide a memory snapshot of the actual parameters before the function is referenced, as well as of the formal parameters at the beginning of the function.

Valid references to the **sinc** function can also include expressions and can include other function references, as shown in the following references to the **sinc** function:

```
cout << sinc(x+2.5) << endl;

cin >> y;
cout << sinc(y) << endl;

z = x*x + sinc(2*x);

w = sinc(fabs(y));
```

In all these references, the formal parameter is still **x**, but the actual parameter is **x+2.5**, or **y**, or **2*x**, or **fabs(y)**, depending on the reference selected.

If a function has more than one parameter, the formal parameters and the actual parameters must match in number, type, and order. A mismatch between the number of formal parameters and the number of actual parameters can be detected by the compiler using the function prototype statement. If the type of an actual parameter is not the same as the type of the corresponding formal parameter, then the value of the actual parameter will be converted to the appropriate type; this conversion is sometimes called **coercion of arguments** and may or may not cause errors. Recall that converting values to a higher type (such as from **float** to **double**) generally works correctly; converting values to a lower type (such as from **float** to **int**) often introduces errors.

Coercion of arguments

Additional errors can be introduced if the actual parameters are out of order. These errors may not be detected by the compiler and can be difficult for you to detect; therefore, be especially careful that the order of the formal parameters and the order of the actual parameters match.

Call-by-value

The function reference in the **sinc** example is a **call-by-value** reference, or a reference by value. In general, a C++ function cannot change the value of an actual parameter. An exception occurs when an actual parameter is an array, and this will be discussed in the next chapter.

Practice!

Consider the following function:

```
//----------------------------------------------------------
//   This function counts positive parameters.

int positive(double a, double b, double c)
{
    int count;

    count = 0;
    if (a >= 0)
        count++;
    if (b >= 0)
        count++;
    if (c >= 0)
        count++;
    return count;
}
//----------------------------------------------------------
```

Assume that the function is referenced with the following statements:

```
x = 25;
total = positive(x, sqrt(x), x-30);
```

1.   Show the memory snapshot of the actual parameters and the formal parameters.

2.   What is the new value of **total**?

STORAGE CLASS AND SCOPE

In the sample programs presented thus far, we have declared variables within a **main** function and within programmer-defined functions. It is also valid to define a variable *before* the **main** function. Therefore, it is important to be able to deter-

Scope

mine the scope of a function or a variable, where **scope** refers to the portion of the program in which it is valid to reference the function or variable; scope is also sometimes defined in terms of the portion of the program in which the function or variable is visible or accessible. Since the scope of a variable is directly related to its **storage class**, we discuss three storage classes: automatic, external, and static.

First, we define the difference between local variables and global variables.

Local variables

Local variables are defined inside a function (including the **main** function) and thus include the formal parameters and any other variables declared in the function. A local variable can be accessed only in the function that defined it. A local variable has a value when its function is being executed, but its value is not

Global variables

retained when the function completes execution. **Global variables** are defined before the **main** function or other programmer-defined functions are defined, so that they can be accessed by any function within the scope of the program; however, to reference a global (or external) variable, a declaration within the function must include the keyword **extern** before the type designation, to tell the compiler to look outside the function for the variable. The **automatic** storage class is the default storage class for local variables, but it can be also be specified with the keyword **auto** before the type designation. The **external** storage class is used to represent global variables; the **extern** designation must be used within functions, and it is optional in the original definition of a global variable.

The memory assigned to an external variable is retained for the duration of execution of the program. Although an external variable can be referenced from a function by means of the proper declaration, using global variables is generally

Style

discouraged. *In general, parameters are preferred for transferring information to a function because the parameter is evident in the function prototype, while an external variable is not visible in the function prototype.*

The storage class of function names is external, and thus a function can be referenced from another function. Function prototypes included outside of any function are also external references and thus are available to all other functions in the program; this explains why we do not need to include **math.h** in every function that references a mathematical function. However, the parameter variables in the function prototype are known only in the function prototype statement.

The **static** storage class is used to specify that the memory for a variable should be retained during the entire execution of a program. Therefore, if a local variable in a function is given a static storage class assignment by using the keyword **static** before its type specification, the variable will not lose its value when the program exits the function in which the variable is defined. A static variable could be used to count the number of times that a function was invoked, since the value of the count would be preserved from one function call to another. In general, the use of global and static variables is discouraged except under special circumstances, because these variables can cause unanticipated "side effects."

CHAPTER SUMMARY

Most programs in C++ benefit from using both library and programmer-defined functions. Functions allow us to reuse software and to employ abstraction in our solution; hence, they reduce development time and increase the quality of the software.

KEY TERMS

abstraction

actual parameter

automatic class

call by value

coercion of arguments

driver

external class

formal parameter

function prototype

global variable

invoke

library function

local variable

modularity

module

programmer-defined function

reusabilitiy

scope

static class

storage class

void

4

C++ STATEMENT SUMMARY

Function Definition:

```
return_type function_name(parameter types)
{
    function body
}
```

Return statements:

```
return;
return (a + b)/2;
```

Function Prototypes:

```
double sinc(double x);
double sinc(double);
void print_data(int x, int y);
```

$\mathcal{STYLE}$ NOTES

1. A program with several modules is easier to read and understand than one long **main** function.
2. Select the name of the function to indicate the purpose of the function.
3. Use a special line, such as a line of dashes, to separate programmer-defined functions from the **main** function and other programmer-defined functions.
4. Use a consistent order for functions, such as the **main** function first, followed by additional functions in the order in which they are referenced.
5. Use parameter identifiers in prototype statements to help document the order and definition of parameters.
6. List function prototypes on separate lines so that they are easy to identify.
7. Use the parameter list instead of external variables to transmit information to a function.

DEBUGGING NOTES

1. If you are having difficulty understanding the error messages from a compiler, try running your program on another compiler to obtain different error messages.
2. When debugging a long program, add comment indicators (//) to sections of the code so that you can focus on other parts of the program.
3. Test a complicated function by itself, using a driver program.
4. Make sure that the value returned from a function matches the function return_type. If necessary, use the cast operator to convert a value to the proper type.
5. Functions can be defined before or after the **main** function, but not within it.
6. Always use function prototype statements to avoid errors in passing parameters.

7. Use **cout** statements to generate memory snapshots of the actual parameters before a function is referenced and of the formal parameters at the beginning of the function.

8. Carefully match the type, order, and number of actual parameters with the type, order, and number of formal parameters of a function.

PROBLEMS

Print Routines. The following problems develop functions that are useful when printing reports. These are all **void** functions because they print information, but do not return any values.

1. Write and test a function that will print your name, course title, and homework number in the following format:

```
Joey Smith
Engineering 101
Homework #5
```

Your name and the course title should be included within the output statements; the homework number is an input parameter. Assume that the function prototype is

```
void header(int hw_number);
```

4

2. Write and test a function that prints two totals in the following format:

```
Summary Information:
    Total 1 xxxx.xx
    Total 2 xxxx.xx
    Combined Totals      xxxxx.xx
```

Assume that the function prototype is

```
void summary(double total_1, double total_2);
```

3. Write and test a function that prints the following error message:

```
Error occurred in the processing of the data file.
Recheck the data before rerunning this program.
```

Assume that the function prototype is

```
void error(void);
```

4. Write and test a function that prints an error message in the following format:

    ```
    Errors occurred in processing the data file.
    xxx values were out of the appropriate range.
    ```

    The number of values out of range is an input parameter to the function. Assume that the function prototype is

    ```
    void error_total(int error_count);
    ```

5. Write and test a function which prints an error message that depends on the value in an integer parameter. If the value of the error flag is 1, print

    ```
    Error identified in the distance data.
    ```

    If the value of the error flag is 2, print

    ```
    Error identified in the velocity data.
    ```

    If the value of the error flag is 3, print

    ```
    Error identified in the acceleration data.
    ```

    For all other values of the error flag, print

    ```
    Unidentified error occurred.
    ```

    Assume that the function prototype is

    ```
    void error_message(int error_flag);
    ```

    Function Evaluations. Functions are often used to evaluate a mathematical function that is not included in the Standard C++ library. The following problems develop functions to return function values.

6. Write and test a function that receives three integers. The function should return the maximum value. Assume that the function prototype is

    ```
    int maximum_int(int a, int b, int c);
    ```

7. Write and test a function that returns the value of $f(x)$, where

    $$f(x) = \frac{3x^2 + x - 2}{x^2 - 2x + 1}$$

    Assume that the function prototype is

    ```
    double f(double x);
    ```

8. Write and test a function that returns the value of $g(x)$, where

    $$g(x) = 0, \qquad x < 0$$

    $$= 6e^{(x-3)}, \quad x \geqslant 0$$

Assume that the function prototype is

```
double g(double x);
```

9. Write and test a function that returns the length of a line from a point (x,y) on a plane to the origin, where

$$\text{length} = \sqrt{x^2 + y^2}$$

Assume that the function prototype is

```
double length(double x, double y);
```

10. Write and test a function that returns the quadrant number of a point (x,y) on a plane. Recall that points in quadrant 1 have positive x and y values, points in quadrant 2 have a negative x value and a positive y value, points in quadrant 3 have negative x and y values, and the remaining points are in quadrant 4. If a point is on an axis, choose the quadrant with the lower quadrant number. Assume that the function prototype is

```
int quadrant(double x, double y);
```

4

Courtesy of FPG International.

GRAND CHALLENGE:
Speech Recognition

The modern jet cockpit has literally hundreds of switches and gauges. Several research programs are investigating the feasibility of using a speech recognition system in the cockpit to serve as a pilot's assistant. The system would respond to verbal requests from the pilot for information such as the fuel status or altitude of the airplane. The pilot would use words from a small vocabulary that the computer had been trained to understand. In addition to understanding a specific vocabulary, the system would have to be trained to "understand" the speech of the pilot who would be using the system. The training information could be stored on a diskette and inserted into the onboard computer at the beginning of a flight so that the system could recognize the current pilot. The computer system would also use speech synthesis to respond to the pilot's request for information.

One-Dimensional Arrays

OBJECTIVES

This chapter introduces the array, a data structure used frequently in solving engineering problems. One-dimensional arrays are discussed in detail, with examples that illustrate defining and initializing arrays, that perform computations with arrays, that use arrays in input and output statements, and that use arrays as function arguments. A set of functions for performing simple statistical measurements on one-dimensional arrays is also developed.

5.1   Array Definitions and Computations

In solving an engineering problem, it is important to be able to visualize the data related to the problem. Sometimes the data consist solely of a single number, such as the radius of a circle. Other times the data may be a coordinate in a plane that can be represented as a pair of numbers, with one number representing the x-coordinate and the other number representing the y-coordinate. There are also times when we want to work with a set of similar data values, but we do not want to give each value a separate name. For example, suppose we have a set of 100 temperature measurements that we want to use to perform several computations. Obviously, we do not want to use 100 different names for the temperature measurements, so we need a method for working with a group of values using a single identifier. One solution to this problem uses a data structure called an **array**.

One-dimensional array

A **one-dimensional array** can be visualized as a list of values arranged in either a row or a column, as follows:

5	0	-1	2	15	2

s[0] s[1] s[2] s[3] s[4] s[5]

t[0]	0.0
t[1]	0.1
t[2]	0.2
t[3]	0.3

Subscripts

We assign an identifier to an array and then distinguish between **elements** or values in the array using **subscripts**. In C++, the subscripts always start with 0 and are incremented by 1. Thus, the first value in the preceding **s** array is referenced by **s[0]**, and the third value in the **t** array is referenced by **t[2]**.

Arrays are convenient for storing and handling large amounts of data, so there is a tendency to use them in algorithms when they are not necessary. Arrays are more complicated to use than simple variables and thus make programs longer and more difficult to debug. Therefore, use arrays only when it is necessary to have the complete set of data available in memory.

DEFINITION AND INITIALIZATION

An array is defined using declaration statements. An integer expression in brackets follows the identifier and specifies the number of elements in the array. Note that all elements in an array must be the same data type. The declaration statements for the foregoing two arrays are as follows:

```
int s[6];
double t[4];
```

An array can be initialized when it is defined, or values can be assigned to it using program statements. To initialize the array at the same time it is defined, the values are specified in a sequence that is separated by commas and enclosed in braces. The following statements define and initialize the previous arrays **s** and **t**:

```
int s[6] = {5, 0, -1, 2, 15, 2};
double t[4] = {0.0, 0.1, 0.2, 0.3};
```

If the initializing sequence is shorter than the array, then the rest of the values are initialized to zero. Hence, the following statement defines an integer array of 100 values, each of which is initialized to zero:

```
int s[100] = {0};
```

If an array is specified without a size, but with an initialization sequence, the size is defined to be equal to the number of values in the sequence. Thus, the following statements also define the arrays **s** and **t**:

```
int s[] = {5, 0, -1, 2, 15, 2};
double t[] = {0.0, 0.1, 0.2, 0.3};
```

The size of an array must be specified in the declaration statement of the array, using either a constant within brackets or an initialization sequence within braces.

Arrays can also be assigned values by means of program statements. For example, suppose that we want to fill a **double** array **g** with the values 0.0, 0.5, 1.0, 1.5, . . . ,10.0. Since there are 21 values, listing the values in the declaration statement of **g** would be tedious. Thus, we use the following statements to define and initialize this array:

```
//  Define variable.
double g[21];
   .
   .
   .
//  Assign initial values to the array g.
for (int k=0; k<21; k++)
   g[k] = k*0.5;
```

It is important to recognize that the condition in the **for** statement must specify a final subscript value of 20, not 21. It is a common mistake to specify a subscript that is one value more than the largest valid subscript, and this error can be very difficult to find because it accesses values outside the array. Since this error is generally not detected during program execution, it is important to be careful about exceeding the array subscripts. In this example, we could also have used the condition **k<=20** instead of **k<21**. *We will generally use* **k** *as the subscript for a one-dimensional array.*

Style

Arrays are often used to store information that is read from data files. For example, suppose we have a data file named **sensor3.dat** that contains 10 time and motion measurements collected from a seismometer with a time and its corresponding motion value on the same line. To read these values into arrays named **time** and **motion**, we could use the following statements that read and store the data using two arrays.

```
//  Define variables.
double time[10], motion[10];
   .
   .
   .
//  Open file and read data into arrays.
fstream sensor3;
sensor3.open("sensor3.dat", ios::in);
for (int k=0; k<10; k++)
   sensor3 >> time[k] >> motion[k];
```

During the first pass through the loop, values are read for **time[0]** and **motion[0]**, during the second pass through the loop, values are read for **time[1]** and **motion[1]**, and so on.

Practice!

Show the contents of the arrays defined in each of the following sets of statements.

1.  ```
    int x[10]={-5, 4, 3};
    ```
2.  ```
    double z[4];
       .
       .
       .
    z[1] = -5.5;
    z[2] = z[3] = fabs(z[1]);
    ```
3.  ```
    double time[9];
       .
       .
       .
    for (int k=0; k<9; k++)
       time[k] = (k-4)*0.1;
    ```

COMPUTATIONS AND I/O

Computations with array elements are specified just like computations with simple variables, but a subscript must be used to specify an individual array element. To illustrate, the following program reads an array **y** of 100 floating-point values
    ```

from a data file. The program determines the average value of the array and stores it in **y_ave**. Then, the number of values in the array **y** that are greater than the average is counted and printed. Note that the number of values to read is declared as a constant **N** and that the rest of the program uses this constant to determine the number of times to execute loops or to determine the value to divide into the sum of the values. This use of a constant then makes the program more flexible, because to change the number of values to be used, we only need to change the value in the symbolic constant.

```
//-------------------------------------------------------------
//   Program chapter5_1
//
//   This program reads 100 values from a data file
//   and determines the number of values greater
//   than the average.

#include <iostream.h>
#include <fstream.h>
#include <stdlib.h>

int main()
{
    //  Define constant and variables.
    const int N=100;
    double y[N], sum=0;

    //  Open file, read data into an array,
    //   and compute a sum of the values.
    fstream lab;
    lab.open("lab1.dat", ios::in);
    for (int k=0; k<N; k++)
    {
        lab >> y[k];
        sum += y[k];
    }

    //  Compute average and count values that
    //   are greater than the average.
    int count=0;
    double y_ave=sum/N;
    for (k=0; k<N; k++)
        if (y[k] > y_ave)
            count++;

    //  Print count.
    cout << count << " values greater than the "
         << "average value" << endl;

    //  Close file and exit program.
    lab.close();
    return EXIT_SUCCESS;
}
//-------------------------------------------------------------
```

If the purpose of this program were to determine the average of the values in the data file, an array would not have been necessary. The loop to read values could read each value into the same variable, adding its value to a sum before the next value is read. However, since we needed to compare each value to the average in order to count the number of values greater than the average, an array was needed so that we could access each value again.

Array values are printed using a subscript to specify the individual value desired. For instance, the following statement prints the first and last values of the array **y** used in the previous example:

```
cout << "first and last array values:" << endl;
     << y[0] << "  " << y[N-1] << endl;
```

The following loop prints all 100 (or **N**) values of **y**, one per line:

```
cout << "y values: " << endl;
for (int k=0; k<N; k++)
   cout << y[k] << endl;
```

When printing a large array, such as this one, we probably would like to print several numbers on the same line. The following statements use the modulus operator to skip to a new line after each group of five values is printed:

```
cout << "y values:" << endl;
for (int k=0; k<N; k++)
   if (k%5 == 0)
      cout << endl << y[k];
   else
      cout << y[k];
cout << endl;
```

Statements similar to the ones illustrated here can also be used to write array values to a data file. For example, the following statement will print the value of **y[k]** on a line in a data file with an object name **sensor**:

```
sensor << y[k] << endl;
```

The next value written to the file will be on a new line.

The number of elements in an array is used in the array declaration and in loops used to access the elements in the array. If the number of elements is changed, then there are several places in the program that need to be modified. *Changing the size of an array is simplified if a symbolic constant is used to specify the size.* Then, to change the size, only the symbolic constant needs to be changed. This style suggestion is especially important in programs that contain many modules or in programming environments in which several programmers are working on the same software project.

Style

Table 5.1 gives an updated precedence order that includes subscript brackets. Brackets and parentheses are associated before the other operators. If parentheses and brackets are nested, the innermost set is evaluated first.

TABLE 5.1 Operator Precedence

Precedence	Operation	Associativity
1	() []	innermost first
2	+ - ++ − cast !	right to left (unary)
3	* / %	left to right
4	+ -	left to right
5	< <= > >=	left to right
6	== !=	left to right
7	&&	left to right
8	||	left to right
9	= += -= *= /= %=	right to left

Practice!

Assume that the array **s** has been defined with the statement

```
int s[]={3, 8, 15, 21, 30, 41};
```

Give the output for each of the following sets of statements.

1.
```
for (int k=0; k<6; k+=2)
    cout << s[k] << "   " << s[k+1] << endl;
```

2.
```
for (int k=0; k<6; k++)
    if (s[k]%2 == 0)
        cout << s[k] << endl;
```

5.2   Arrays as Function Arguments

When the information in an array is passed to a function, two parameters are usually used; one parameter specifies the specific array, and the other parameter specifies the number of elements used in the array. By specifying the number of elements of the array that are to be used, the function becomes more flexible. For example, if the function specifies an integer array, then the function can be used with any integer array; the parameter that specifies the number of elements assures that we use the correct size. Also, the number of elements used in an array may vary from one time to another. For example, the array may use elements read from a data file; the number of elements then depends on the specific data file used when the program is executed. In all these examples, though, the array must be declared to be a maximum size in the **main** function, and then the actual number of elements used can be less than or equal to that maximum size.

Consider the following program, which reads an array from a data file and then references a function to determine the maximum value in the array. The variable **npts** is used to specify the number of values in the array; the value of **npts** can be less than or equal to the defined size of the array, which is 100. The function has two arguments—the name of the array and the number of points in the array, as indicated in the function prototype statement.

```cpp
//-------------------------------------------------------------
//  Program chapter5_2
//
//  This program reads values from a data file and
//  determines the maximum value with a function.

#include <iostream.h>
#include <fstream.h>
#include <stdlib.h>

int main()
{
    //  Define constant, variables, and prototype.
    const int N=100;
    int npts;
    double y[N];
    double array_max(double x[], int n);

    //  Input the number of data values.
    cout << "Enter the number of data values: ";
    cin >> npts;

    //  Open file and read data into an array.
    fstream lab;
    lab.open("lab1.dat", ios::in);
    for (int k=0; k<npts; k++)
       lab >> y[k];

    //  Find and print the maximum value.
    cout << "maximum value: "
         << array_max(y,npts) << endl;

    //  Close file and exit program.
    lab.close();
    return EXIT_SUCCESS;
}
//-------------------------------------------------------------
//  This function returns the maximum
//  value in the array x with n elements.
//
double array_max(double x[], int n)
{
    //  Define variable.
    double max_x;

    //  Determine the maximum value in the array.
    max_x = x[0];
    for (int k=1; k<n; k++)
       if (x[k] > max_x)
          max_x = x[k];

    //  Return maximum value.
    return max_x;
}
//-------------------------------------------------------------
```

The program assumes that there will be no more than 100 values in the file; otherwise, it will not work correctly. Arrays must be specified to be as large as, or larger than, the maximum number of values to be read into them.

The purpose of program **chapter 5_2** was to illustrate the use of an array as a function argument. If the purpose of the program were to determine the maximum of the data values in the file, an array would not have been necessary; the maximum could have been determined as the data values were read.

CALL-BY-ADDRESS REFERENCES

There is a very significant difference between using arrays as parameters and using simple variables as parameters. When a simple variable is used as a parameter, the value is passed to the formal parameter in the function, and thus, the original value cannot be changed; this is a call-by-value reference. When an array is used as a parameter, the memory address of the array is passed to the function, instead of the entire set of values in the array. Therefore, the function references values in the original array; this is a **call-by-address** reference. Because a function accesses the original array values, we must be very careful that we do not inadvertently change values in an array within a function. Of course, there may also be occasions when we wish to change the values in the array.

Call-by-address

Practice!

Assume that the following variables are defined:

```
int k=6;
double data[]={1.5, 3.2, -6.1, 9.8, 8.7, 5.2};
```

Give the values of the following expressions that reference the **array_max** function presented in this section.

1. **array_max(data,6);**
2. **array_max(data,5);**
3. **array_max(data,k-3);**
4. **array_max(data,k%5);**

STATISTICAL MEASUREMENTS

Analyzing data collected from engineering experiments is an important part of evaluating the experiments. This analysis ranges from simple computations on the data, such as calculating the average value, to more complicated compu-tations. Many of the computations or measurements using data are statistical measurements because they have statistical properties that change from one set of data to another. For example, the sine of 60° is an exact value that is the same every time we compute it, but the number of miles to the gallon that we get with our car is a statistical measurement because it varies somewhat, depending on parameters such as the temperature, the speed that we travel, the type of road we are on, and whether we are in the mountains or the desert.

When evaluating a set of experimental data, we often compute the maxi-mum value, minimum value, mean or average value, and median. In this section, we develop functions that can be used to compute these values using an array as input. These functions will be useful in solutions to problems at the end of the chapter. It is important to note that the functions assume that there is at least one value in the array.

Maximum, Minimum. A function for determining the maximum value in an array was presented earlier in this section; a similar function can easily be developed for determining the minimum value.

Mean

Average. The Greek symbol μ (mu) is used to represent the average or **mean** value, as shown in the following equation, which uses summation notation:

$$\mu = \frac{\sum_{k=0}^{n-1} x_k}{n} \qquad (5.1)$$

Here, $\sum_{k=0}^{n-1} x_k = x_0 + x_1 + x_2 + \ldots + x_{n-1}$. The average of a set of values is always a floating-point value, even if all the data values are integers. The following func-tion computes the mean value of a **double** array of n values:

```
//-----------------------------------------------------------
//   This function returns the average or
//   mean value of an array with n elements.
//
double array_mean(double x[], int n)
{
    //  Define and initialize variable.
    double sum=0;

    //  Determine mean value.
    for (int k=0; k<n; k++)
        sum += x[k];

    //  Return mean value.
    return sum/n;
}
//-----------------------------------------------------------
```

Note that the variable **sum** was initialized to zero in the declaration statement. It could also have been initialized to zero with an assignment statement. In either case, the value of **sum** is initialized to zero each time that the function is referenced.

Median

Median. The **median** is the value in the middle of a group of values, assuming that the values are sorted. If there is an odd number of values, the median is precisely the value in the middle; if there is an even number of values, the median is the average of the values in the two middle positions. For example, the median of the values {1, 6, 18, 39, 86} is the middle value, or 18; the median of the values {1, 6, 18, 39, 86, 91} is the average of the two middle values, or $(18 + 39)/2$, or 28.5. Assume that a group of sorted values is stored in an array and that **n** contains the number of values in the array. If **n** is odd, then the subscript of the middle value can be represented by **floor(n/2)**, as in **floor(5/2)**, which is 2. If **n** is even, then the subscripts of the two middle values can be represented by **floor(n/2)-1** and **floor(n/2)**, as in **floor(6/2)-1** and **floor(6/2)**, which are 2 and 3, respectively, using the preceding example. The following function determines the median of a set of values stored in an array. We assume that the values are sorted (into either ascending or descending order).

```
//-------------------------------------------------------
//   This function returns the median
//   value in an array x with n elements.
//
double array_median(double x[], int n)
{
    //   Define variable.
    double median_x;

    //   Determine median value.
    int k = floor(n/2);
    if (n%2 != 0)
        median_x = x[k];
    else
        median_x = (x[k-1] + x[k])/2;

    //   Return median value.
    return median_x;
}
//-------------------------------------------------------
```

Go through the function by hand, using the two sets of data values given in this discussion.

CHAPTER SUMMARY

An array is a data structure often used to store engineering data that are best represented by a list of information. Examples were developed in this chapter to illustrate array definitions, array initializations, computations with arrays, input and output with arrays, and arrays as function parameters. A set of simple statistical functions was developed for analyzing one-dimensional arrays.

KEY TERMS

array	median
call by address	one-dimensional array
element	subscript
mean	

C++ STATEMENT SUMMARY

Array Definition:

```
int a[5], b[]={2, 3, -1};
```

STYLE NOTES

1. The variable **k** is commonly used as a subscript (index) for a one-dimensional array.
2. Use symbolic constants to declare the size of an array so that it is easy to modify.

DEBUGGING NOTES

1. Use arrays only when it is necessary to keep all the data available in memory.
2. Be careful not to exceed the maximum subscript value when referencing an element in an array.
3. An array must be declared to be as large as, or larger than, the maximum number of values to be stored in it.
4. Since an array reference in a function is a call-by-address reference, be careful that you do not inadvertently change values in an array in the function.

PROBLEMS

The following problems are all stated in terms of writing a function that has an array as an argument. Alternative problems can be defined that do not require functions by changing each problem to one involving reading 20 values from the keyboard and storing them in an array. The program should then determine and print the value computed as an array characteristic (Problems 1–5) or modify and print the array values (Problems 6–10).

Array Characteristics. It is very convenient to have a group of functions for determining information stored in an array. The functions **array_max**, **array_mean**, and **array_median** developed in this chapter are examples of these types of routines. The following problems develop additional functions that are useful for working with arrays.

1.   Write and test a function that will determine whether the values in an array are in ascending order (adjacent values are increasing or equal in value) or descending order (adjacent values are decreasing or equal in value). The function value should be 1 if the array values are in ascending order, -1 if they are in descending order, and 0 if they are in neither order. Assume that the function prototype is

```
int order(int x[], int npts);
```

2.   Write and test a function that will compare values in two arrays of the same size. If the values are the same, the function should return a 1; otherwise it should return a 0. Assume that the function prototype is

```
int identical(int a[], int b[], int npts);
```

3.   Write and test a function that counts the number of values in an array that are greater than a specified target value. Assume that the function prototype is

```
int greater_count(int x[], int npts, int target);
```

4.   Write and test a function that counts the number of values in an array that are less than or equal to a specified target value. Use the function developed in Problem 3 in your solution. Assume that the function prototype is

```
int less_equal_count(int x[], int npts, int target);
```

5.   Write and test a function that determines the largest difference between two adjacent values in an array. If there is only one value in the array, the difference should be zero. Assume that the function prototype is

```
double diff(double y[], int npts);
```

Array Modification. The following set of functions modifies the values in an array.

6. Suppose that an array contains angles in radians. Write a function that converts the radian measure to degrees. Assume that the function prototype is

```
void rad_to_deg(double b[], int npts);
```

7. Suppose that an array contains angles in degrees. Write a function that converts any angles outside of the interval [0,360] to an equivalent angle in that interval. For example, an angle of 380.5 degrees should be converted to 20.5 degrees. Assume that the function prototype is

```
void reduce_angle(double b[], int npts);
```

8. Write and test a function that will replace (or "clip") any value above a specified value with the specified value. Assume that the function prototype is

```
void clip(double b[], int npts, double peak_value);
```

To illustrate, the following function reference will replace any value above 5.0 in the array **x** with the value 5.0:

```
clip(x, n, 5.0);
```

9. Write and test a function that will subtract the mean value of an array from each element in the array. (The mean value of these new values is then always zero.) Use the function **array_mean** in your function. Assume that the function prototype is

```
void remove_mean(double x[], int npts);
```

10. There are a number of ways to normalize, or scale, a set of values. One common normalization technique scales the values such that the minimum value goes to 0, the maximum value goes to 1, and other values are scaled accordingly. Using this technique, we can normalize the values in the top array to the values shown in the bottom array:

Array values:

-2	-1	2	0

Normalized array values:

0.0	0.25	1.0	0.5

The equation that computes the normalized value from a value x_k in the top array is

$$\text{normalized } x_k = \frac{x_k - \min_x}{\max_x - \min_x}$$

where $\min_x$ and $\max_x$ represent the minimum and maximum values in the array x. If you substitute the minimum value for x_k in this equation, the numerator is zero, and thus the normalized value for the minimum is zero. If you substitute the maximum value for x_k in the equation, the numerator and denominator are the same, and hence the normalized value for the maximum is 1.0. Write and test a function that has a one-dimensional **double** array and the number of values in the array as its arguments. Normalize the values in the array using the technique just presented. Use the function **array_max** that was developed in this chapter and a similar function **array_min**. Assume that the function prototype is

```
void norm(double x[], int npts);
```

5

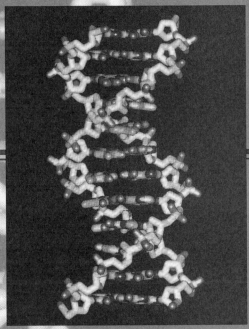

Courtesy of Photo Researchers, Inc.

GRAND CHALLENGE:
Mapping the Human Genome

The deciphering of the human genetic code involves locating, identifying, and determining the functions of each of the 50,000 to 100,000 genes that are contained in human DNA. Each gene is a double-helix strand composed of base pairs of adenine bonded with thymine, or cytosine bonded with guanine, that are arranged in a steplike manner with phosphate groups along the side. DNA directs the production of proteins, so the proteins produced by a cell provide a key to the sequence of base pairs in the DNA. Instrumentation developed for genetic engineering is extremely useful in this detective work. A protein sequencer developed in 1969 can identify the sequence of amino acids in a protein molecule. Once the amino acid order is known, biologists can begin to identify the gene that made the protein. A DNA synthesizer, developed in 1982, can build small genes or gene fragments out of DNA. This research and its associated instrumentation are key components in the quest to map the human genome.

Character Data

OBJECTIVES

Character information is an important type of information to represent and manipulate in solving engineering problems. Each character is stored using a binary code; because it is the most commonly used code, the ASCII representation is discussed in detail in this chapter. Examples are presented to demonstrate that character information can be processed as character data types or as integers that correspond to the ASCII code values. The initialization of character variables is discussed, and new I/O statements are presented for reading and printing characters. A number of functions from the Standard C++ library that work with characters are presented, and functions are developed that use characters as arguments.

6.1   Character Information

Numeric information is represented in a C++ program as integers or floating-point values. Numeric values can be single, independent values, or they can be grouped together in an array. Often, they are used in arithmetic computations. In many solutions, however, we also need to store and manipulate nonnumeric information (**characters**), which may consist of alphabetic characters, digits, and special characters. Even though nonnumeric information can contain digits, the digits are not values generally used in arithmetic computations; instead, they may be digits in an address, a phone number, or a social security number.

Recall that all information stored in a computer is represented internally as sequences of binary digits (0 and 1). In general, we do not need to be concerned about this binary representation, because the compiler and the computer perform the necessary steps to convert our programs to binary and then to execute them. However, in order to work with characters, we need to understand more about their representation in the computer's memory. Each character corresponds to a binary code value. The most commonly used **binary codes** are **ASCII** (American Standard Code for Information Interchange) and **EBCDIC** (Extended Binary Coded Decimal Interchange Code). In the discussions that follow, we assume that ASCII code is used to represent characters. Table 6.1 contains a few characters, their binary form in ASCII, and the integer values that correspond to the binary values. Thus, the character **a** is represented by the binary value 1100001, which is equivalent to an integer value of 97. A total of 128 characters can be represented in ASCII; a complete ASCII code table is given in Appendix A.

ASCII

Once a character is stored in memory as a binary value, the binary value can be interpreted as a character or an integer, as illustrated in Table 6.1. Thus, when we define variables that are to be used for storing characters, we can define them as either characters or integers. However, it is important to note that the binary representation of a character digit is not equal to the binary representation of an integer digit. For example, from the table, we see that the binary representation of the digit 3 is equivalent to the binary representation of the integer 51. Thus, performing a computation with the character representation of a digit does not yield the same result as performing the computation with the integer representation of the digit.

TABLE 6.1 Examples of ASCII Codes

Character	ASCII Code	Integer Equivalent
new line, \n	0001010	10
%	0100101	37
3	0110011	51
A	1000001	65
a	1100001	97
b	1100010	98
c	1100011	99

Nonnumeric information can be represented by constants or by variables in our programs. A character constant is enclosed in single quotes, as in **'A'**, **'b'**, or **'3'**. A variable that is to contain a character is defined as a character data type **(char)**. Character arrays can be used to represent a group of characters. C++ also allows the definition of a character string, but character strings are not discussed in this text.

Practice!

Using the ASCII code table from Appendix A, give integer values for the following characters.

1. **(**   2. **<**
3. **G**   4. **g**

Give the ASCII characters (or meaning) that correspond to each of the following binary code values.

5. 1001111   6. 0100100
7. 1110101   8. 1011110

6.2   Character Initialization and Computations

The binary representation of a character can be interpreted as a character or an integer. The following statements illustrate printing an integer value that is also assigned to a character variable:

```
//  Define and initialize variables.
int k=97;
char c=k;

//  Print the value 97 as an integer and character.
cout << "value of k: " << k
     << "; value of c: " << c << endl;
```

The output from these statements is

```
value of k: 97; value of c: a
```

A similar set of statements illustrates printing a character value that is also assigned to an integer variable:

```
//  Define and initialize variables.
char c='b';
int k=c;
```

```
//  Print the value 'b' as a character and integer.
cout << "value of k: " << k
     << "; value of c: " << c << endl;
```

The output of these statements is

```
value of k: 98; value of c: b
```

CHARACTER I/O

Although the **cout** and **cin** statements can be used to read and print characters, C++ also contains special functions for reading and printing characters. The **get** function reads a character from the keyboard and assigns it to the specified variable; the **put** function prints a character to the computer screen. The prototype statements for these functions are:

```
cout.put(char_name);
cin.get(char_name);
```

For example, the following program segment reads a single character from the keyboard and prints the character on the screen by using the **get** and **put** functions:

```
char grade;
cout << "Enter the grade (A,B,C,D or F): ";
cin.get(grade);
cout << "Display the grade: ";
cout.put(grade);
     .
     .
     .
```

A sample output from these statements is

```
Enter the grade (A,B,C,D or F): A
Display the grade: A
```

Text stream

Both the **get** function and the **put** function use a **text stream** composed of a sequence of characters. For the **get** function, the text stream is the line entered through the keyboard; for the **put** function, the text stream is the line printed on the screen. In either case, the text stream can be separated into lines by newline characters. The end of a text stream is indicated with the special end-of-file value,

EOF

EOF. This special value is a symbolic constant defined in the header file **stdio.h**. (Recall that we used this value to detect the end of a data file in Chapter 3.)

Execution of the **put** function causes a character to be written to the computer screen. If several **put** function references are made in a row, the characters are printed one after another on the same line, until the end of the line is specified. Thus, the following statements cause the characters **ab** to be printed on one line, followed by **c** on the next line:

```
cout.put('a');
cout.put('b');
cout.put('\n');
cout.put('c');
```

The same information could be printed using the integer values that correspond to the characters (see Table 6.1):

```
cout.put(97);
cout.put(98);
cout.put(10);
cout.put(99);
```

Style

In general, we prefer to use character constants instead of their binary equivalents in order to make the program easier to read.

When a **get** function is executed, the next character in the current input text stream is obtained, and the function returns 1 (for "true") if the character is not the **EOF** character and 0 (for "false") otherwise. If there is no current text stream, then a line of information is obtained from the keyboard. This line must be ended by pressing the return key, which corresponds to entering a newline character. Thus, when the first **get** function is executed in a program, a line of information is read from the keyboard, but only the first character in the line is returned by the function. When the next **get** function reference is executed, the second character from the same line is returned by the function. Successive references continue to return additional characters, until the character returned is a newline character; this signifies that we have reached the end of the current line. Then, the next reference to the **get** function causes a new line of information to be read from the keyboard into the text stream. This processing of the text stream by lines continues until the **EOF** character is entered through the keyboard. (The **get** function will return 0 if the **EOF** character is encountered.)

The value of the **EOF** character is system dependent; in the Borland Turbo C++ environment, the **EOF** character is entered by pressing the control (ctrl) key and then pressing the z key while the control key is still pressed. This combination of characters is often written as ^z, but this is not the same as pressing the ^ key followed by the z key. In the Borland Turbo C++ environment, the **EOF** character is represented internally by the integer value −1. (Note that you cannot enter −1 for the **EOF** character, because it will be interpreted as a minus sign followed by the digit 1.) The sequence of characters that represents the **EOF** character on many UNIX systems is ^d. To determine the sequence of characters that represents the **EOF** character on other systems, consult your instructor or a computing center consultant.

To illustrate the use of the **get** and **put** functions, consider the following program, which reads characters from the keyboard and prints them to the screen. The program also computes and prints a count of the characters read, including spaces and newline characters, but not including the **EOF** character. Note that the user is reminded of the sequence necessary to terminate the text stream.

```
//-------------------------------------------------------------
//  Program chapter6_1
//
//  This program demonstrates the relationship
//  between a text stream and character I/O by
//  reading characters from the keyboard and then
//  printing them to the screen.

#include <iostream.h>
#include <stdlib.h>

int main()
{
   //  Define and initialize variables.
   int count=0;
   char c;

   //  Read, print, and count characters.
   cout << "Enter characters (^z to quit):" << endl;
   while (cin.get(c))
   {
      cout.put(c);
      count++;
   }

   //  Print the number of characters printed.
   cout << count << " characters printed" << endl;

   //  Exit program.
   return EXIT_SUCCESS;
}
//-------------------------------------------------------------
```

The **while** loop condition uses the value returned by the **get** function in order to continue the loop until the **EOF** character is read (and 0 is returned).

When the first **get** function is executed, a line of text is obtained from the keyboard. (Note that this line of text must be ended by pressing the return key, which is equivalent to a newline character.) The first reference to the **get** function reads only the first character of the line and assigns it to the variable **c**, but successive executions of the **get** function cause additional characters on the line to be read and assigned. Therefore, you may enter as many characters as you want on a line, but processing of the program will not continue until you press the return (or enter) key.

An example of the information displayed on the screen during a sample execution of Program **chapter6_1** is the following:

```
Enter characters (^z to quit):
abcd
abcd
z
z
```

```
1w2e3r $
1w2e3r $
^z
16 characters printed
```

The first line of characters was **abcd** followed by a new line, the second line contained the character **z** followed by a new line, and the third line contained the characters **1w2e3r $** followed by a new line. The fourth line contained the **EOF** representation followed by a new line; the **EOF** representation caused the program to be terminated. Thus, a total of $5 + 2 + 9 + 1$, or 17, characters were read, but only 16 were printed.

A variation of program **chapter6_1** is shown in the next program, which prints each character twice and also counts the number of lines read.

```cpp
//-------------------------------------------------------------
//   Program chapter6_2
//
//   This program reads characters from the keyboard
//   and prints them twice on the screen.  It also
//   counts and prints the number of lines read.

#include <iostream.h>
#include <stdlib.h>

int main()
{
   // Define constants and variables.
   const char NEWLINE='\n';
   int count=0;
   char c;

   // Read and print characters.
   cout << "Enter characters (^z to quit):" << endl;
   while (cin.get(c))
   {
      cout.put(c);
      cout.put(c);
      if (c == NEWLINE)       // Count the lines.
         count++;
   }

   // Print the number of lines read.
   cout << count << " lines read" << endl;

   // Exit program.
   return EXIT_SUCCESS;
}
//-------------------------------------------------------------
```

A sample output from this program, using the same input as for the previous program, is as follows:

```
Enter characters (^z to quit):
abcd
aabbccdd

z
zz

1w2e3r $
11ww22ee33rr   $$

^z
3 lines read
```

Note that the extra line following each line of output is generated by the duplication of the newline character at the end of each input line.

CHARACTER ARRAYS

A group of characters can be stored in a character array. Individual characters in a character array are accessed using subscripts. Character arrays can also be used as function arguments. To illustrate, we present a program that counts the number of words in a data file containing text. We assume that words are not split between lines and that there is at least one blank between words. We also assume that the maximum number of characters on a line, including the newline character, is 100. Each character can be read using the **get** function with the general form

```
object_name.get(char_name)
```

where **object_name** refers to the file object. This function reads characters from a text stream in a data file and returns a value of 1 until the end of the text stream is reached. The program is as follows:

```
//-----------------------------------------------------------
//  Program chapter6_3
//
//  This program reads characters from a data file
//  and counts the number of words, line by line.

#include <iostream.h>
#include <fstream.h>
#include <stdlib.h>

int main()
{
   // Define constant, variables, and prototypes.
   const char NEWLINE='\n';
   int k=0, count=0;
   char line[100];
   int word_ct(char x[], int npts);

   // Open file.
   fstream text1;
   text1.open("text1.dat", ios::in);
```

```
   //  Read characters and count words.
   while (text1.get(line[k]))
   {
      if (line[k] == NEWLINE)
      {
         if (k != 0)  // line is not blank
            count += word_ct(line,k);
         k = 0;
      }
      else  // get next character
         k++;
   }

   //  Count words in the last line of data.
   if (k != 0)
      count += word_ct(line,k);

   //  Print number of words read.
   cout << count << " words read" << endl;

   //  Close file and exit program.
   text1.close();
   return EXIT_SUCCESS;
}
//------------------------------------------------------------
//  This function counts the number of words
//  in a character array.

int word_ct(char x[], int npts)
{
   //  Define and initialize variables.
   int count=0, k=0;

   //  While not at the end of the array,
   //  look for the first character of a word.
   while (k < npts)
   {
      while (k<=npts-1 && x[k]==' ')  // skip blanks
         k++;
      if (k < npts)  // not at end of array
         count++;
      while (k<npts && x[k]!=' ')  // skip letters
         k++;
   }

   //  Return word count.
   return count;
}
//------------------------------------------------------------
```

By using a function to count the number of words in a line, we are able to keep the **main** function short and readable. When the function finds the beginning of a word, it increments the word count. The end of the word is then determined by finding another space or reaching the end of the array. This program was executed with a data file containing the chapter-opening discussion on the human genome; the output from the program gave the correct word count of 166. Note that in order to get characters from the data file, the file object name must be connected to the **get** function through a period, ".". One of the advantages of C++ is that it allows us to connect a file object to the function needed, such as **cin**, **cout**, or a file object name.

CHARACTER COMPARISONS

A character can be compared with another character. It is clear that the values of characters are equal if they are the same character. However, suppose **a** and **b** are character variables and we evaluate the condition **a<b**. At first it may seem strange to ask whether one character is less than another character, but if we consider the comparison in terms of the integer values represented by the characters, then the comparison makes sense. If we want to know whether **'?' < 'A'**, we simply need to refer to the ASCII code table in Appendix A. Since the numeric value of **'?'** is 63, and the numeric value of **'A'** is 65, the comparison is true.

Collating sequence

The ordering of characters in a specific code, from low to high, is a **collating sequence**. If you study the ASCII collating sequence in Appendix A, you may observe some interesting characteristics. The character codes for the digits 0 through 9 are contiguous, the character codes for the uppercase letters A through Z are contiguous, and the character codes for the lowercase letters a through z are contiguous. Also, digits are less than uppercase letters, which are less than lowercase letters. The difference between an uppercase letter and its corresponding lowercase letter is 32. Finally, special characters are not contiguous: Some special characters are before digits, others are after digits, and still others are between uppercase and lowercase letters.

Consider the following program, which counts the number of digits in an input text stream:

```
//-------------------------------------------------------------
//   Program chapter6_4
//
//   This program counts and prints the
//   number of digits in an input text stream.

#include <iostream.h>
#include <stdlib.h>

int main()
{
   // Define and initialize variables.
   int count=0;
   char c;

   // Read characters and count digits.
   cout << "Enter characters (^z to quit):" << endl;
   while (cin.get(c))
      if ('0'<=c && c<='9')
         count++;
```

```
    //  Print the number of digits read.
    cout << count << " digits read" << endl;

    //  Exit program.
    return EXIT_SUCCESS;
}
//-----------------------------------------------------------
```

A sample interaction with this program is the following:

```
Enter characters: (^z to quit)
514 East Sixth St.
Hampton, NH 30255-0345
^z
12 digits read
```

An alternative to Program **chapter6_4** is developed in the next section.

6.3   Character Functions

The Standard C++ library contains a set of functions for use with characters. These functions fall into two categories: One set of functions is used to convert characters between uppercase and lowercase, and the other set is used to perform comparisons between characters. Each function requires a character argument and returns an integer value; the prototype statements for the functions are included in the header file **ctype.h**. The character comparison functions return a nonzero value if the comparison is true; otherwise, they return a zero.

tolower(c)	If **c** is an uppercase letter, this function returns the corresponding lowercase letter; otherwise it returns **c**.
toupper(c)	If **c** is a lowercase letter, this function returns the corresponding uppercase letter; otherwise it returns **c**.
isdigit(c)	This function returns a nonzero value if **c** is a decimal digit; otherwise it returns a zero.
islower(c)	This function returns a nonzero value if **c** is a lowercase letter; otherwise it returns a zero.
isupper(c)	This function returns a nonzero value if **c** is an uppercase letter; otherwise it returns a zero.
isalpha(c)	This functions returns a nonzero value if **c** is an uppercase letter or a lowercase letter; otherwise it returns a zero.
isalnum(c)	This function returns a nonzero value if **c** is an **alphanumeric character** (an alphabetic character or a numeric digit); otherwise it returns a zero.
iscntrl(c)	This function returns a nonzero value if **c** is a control character; otherwise it returns a zero. (The **control characters** have ASCII integer codes of 0 through 21 and 127.)

`isgraph(c)`	This function returns a nonzero value if `c` is a character that can be printed, as opposed to a character that cannot be printed, such as a space, a control character, or a tab; otherwise the function returns a zero. (The printing characters have ASCII integer codes from 32 through 126.)
`isprint(c)`	This function returns a nonzero value if `c` is a printing character (including the space character); otherwise it returns a zero.
`ispunct(c)`	This function returns a nonzero value if `c` is a printing character, with the exception of a space, a letter, or a digit; otherwise it returns a zero.
`isspace(c)`	This function returns a nonzero value if `c` is a space, form feed, new line, carriage return, horizontal tab, or vertical tab (these characters are also referred to as **white space**); otherwise the function returns a zero.
`isxdigit(c)`	This function returns a nonzero value if `c` is a hexadecimal digit, which is a decimal digit or an alphabetic character A through F (or a through f); otherwise the function returns a zero.

Style

All of the preceding functions perform operations similar to some of the operations that we included in previous programs. *In general, use a library function when possible, instead of writing your own statements;* this reduces the length of your programs and also reduces debugging time.

We now rewrite program **chapter6_4** so that it uses a library character function to determine the number of digits in an input text stream. (Note that an additional **include** statement is needed.)

```
//------------------------------------------------------------
//   Program chapter6_5
//
//   This program counts and prints the
//   number of digits in an input text stream.

#include <iostream.h>
#include <stdlib.h>
#include <ctype.h>

int main()
{
   // Define and initialize variables.
   int count=0;
   char c;

   //  Read characters and count digits.
   cout << "Enter characters (^z to quit):" << endl;
   while (cin.get(c))
      if (isdigit(c))
         count++;
```

```
    //  Print the number of digits read.
    cout << count << " digits read" << endl;

    //  Exit program.
    return EXIT_SUCCESS;
}
//-------------------------------------------------------------
```

The sample output with this program is same as with program **chapter6_4**.

CHAPTER SUMMARY

Using the ASCII binary code to represent characters, we presented techniques for initializing, manipulating, and printing character information. The variables containing the character information were defined as integers and then referenced as either integers or characters, depending on the problem to be solved. Examples were presented that used character information as function arguments.

KEY TERMS

alphanumeric character

ASCII code

binary code

character

collating sequence

control character

EBCDIC code

EOF character

text stream

white space

C++ STATEMENT SUMMARY

Include character function header file:

```
#include <ctype.h>
```

Declare and initialize character variable:

```
char c = '*';
```

Declare character array:

```
char line[100];
```

Read character from the keyboard:

```
cin.get(c)
```

6

Read character from a data file:

```
text1.get(line[k])
```

Print character to the screen:

```
cout.put(c)
```

Write character to a data file:

```
text2.put(line[k])
```

STYLE NOTES

1. Use character constants instead of their binary equivalents in program statements.
2. Use character library functions instead of writing similar ones yourself.

DEBUGGING NOTES

1. Remember that the integer representation of a character digit is not the same as the integer representation of the corresponding numerical digit.
2. To reduce the debugging time of your program, use character library functions instead of writing similar ones yourself.

PROBLEMS

Data Filters. Programs called data filters are often used to read the information in a data file and then analyze the contents. In many cases, the data filter program is designed to remove any data errors that would cause problems with other programs that read the information from the data file. The following programs are designed to perform error checking and data analysis on information in a data file. Use an editor or a word processor to generate text files to test all features of the programs.

1. Write a program which reads a data file that should contain only integer values and thus should contain only digits, plus or minus signs, and white space. The program should print any invalid characters located in the file, and at the end it should print a count of the invalid characters located.

2. Write a program that analyzes a data file that has been determined to contain only integer values and white space. The program should print the number of lines in the file and the number of integer values (not integer digits).

3. Write a program that reads a file that contains only integers, some of which have embedded commas, as in 145,020. The program should copy the information to a new file, removing any commas from the information. Do not change the number of values per line in the file.

Bar Graphs. Characters can be used to print a bar graph that corresponds to a set of numerical values. For example, the following bar graph corresponds to the integers 5,9,2,4,10,7:

```
5    *****
9    *********
2    **
4    ****
10   **********
7    *******
```

4. Write a function that receives an integer array and an integer variable that contains the number of integer values in the array. If all the values are between 0 and 50, print a bar graph similar to the one just shown, and return a value of 0; otherwise, do not print a bar graph, and return a value of 1. Assume that the corresponding function prototype statement is

    ```
    int bargraph_1(int count, int data[]);
    ```

Cryptography. The science of developing secret codes (cryptography) has interested many people for centuries. Some of the simplest codes involve replacing a character or a group of characters with another character or group of characters, respectively. To decode these messages easily, the decoder needs a key that shows the replacement characters. In recent times, computers have been used very successfully to decode many codes that initially were assumed to be unbreakable. The next set of problems considers simple codes and schemes for decoding them. Generate files to test the programs.

5. A simple code can be developed by replacing each character by another character that is a fixed number of positions away in the collating sequence. For example, if each character is replaced by the character that is two characters to the right in the collating sequence, then the letter 'a' is replaced by the letter 'c', the letter 'b' is replaced by the letter 'd', and so on. Using this scheme, write a program that reads the text in a file and then generates a new file that contains the coded text. Do not change newline characters or the **EOF** character.

6. Write a program to decode the scheme presented in Problem 5, assuming that you know the coding scheme. Test the program using files generated by Problem 5.

7. One step in breaking a simple code such as the one described in Problem 5 when you do not know the coding scheme involves counting the number of occurrences of each character. Then, knowing that the most common

6

letter in English is 'e', the letter that occurs most commonly in the coded message is replaced by 'e'. Similar replacements are then made based on the number of occurrences of characters in the coded message and the known occurrences of characters in the English language. This decoding often provides enough of the correct replacements that the incorrect replacements can then be determined. Write a program that reads a data file and determines the number of occurrences of each of the characters in the file. Then print the characters and the number of times that they occurred. (*Hint*: Use an array to store the occurrences of the characters, based on their ASCII codes.)

8. Another simple code encodes a message in text such that the true message is represented by the first letter of each word. Write a program to read a data file and determine the secret message stored by the sequence of first letters of the words. Note that there will be no spaces between the words in the secret message, but the decoded string of characters can easily be separated into words by a person.

9. Write a program that encodes the text in a data file using a character array named **key** that contains 26 characters. This key is read from the keyboard; the first letter contains the character that is to replace the letter a in the data file, the second letter contains the letter that is to replace the letter b in the data file, and so on. Assume that all punctuation is to be replaced by spaces. Check to be sure that the key does not map two different characters to the same one during the encoding.

10. Write a program which decodes the file that is the output of Program 9. Assume that the same character **key** is read from the keyboard by the new program and is used in the decoding steps. Note that you will not be able to restore the punctuation characters.

Appendix A
ASCII Character Codes

The following table contains the 128 ASCII characters and their equivalent integer and binary values. The characters that correspond to the integers 1 through 31 have special significance to the computer system. For example, the character BEL, represented by the integer 7, causes the bell to sound on the keyboard.

The order of the characters from low to high represents the collating sequence and has several interesting characteristics. Note that the digits are less than uppercase letters, and uppercase letters are less than lowercase letters. Note also that special characters are not grouped together; some are before digits, some are after digits, and some are between uppercase and lowercase characters.

Character		Integer Equivalent	Binary Equivalent
NUL	(Blank)	000	0000000
SOH	(Start of Header)	001	0000001
STX	(Start of Text)	002	0000010
ETX	(End of Text)	003	0000011
EOT	(End of Transmission)	004	0000100
ENQ	(Enquiry)	005	0000101
ACK	(Acknowledge)	006	0000110
BEL	(Bell)	007	0000111
BS	(Backspace)	008	0001000
HT	(Horizontal Tab)	009	0001001
LF	(Line Feed or New Line)	010	0001010
VT	(Vertical Tabulation)	011	0001011
FF	(Form Feed)	012	0001100
CR	(Carriage Return)	013	0001101
SO	(Shift Out)	014	0001110
SI	(Shift In)	015	0001111
DLE	(Data Link Escape)	016	0010000
DC1	(Device Control 1)	017	0010001
DC2	(Device Control 2)	018	0010010
DC3	(Device Control 3)	019	0010011
DC4	(Device Control 4-Stop)	020	0010100
NAK	(Negative Acknowledge)	021	0010101
SYN	(Synchronization)	022	0010110
ETB	(End of Text Block)	023	0010111
CAN	(Cancel)	024	0011000
EM	(End of Medium)	025	0011001
SUB	(Substitute)	026	0011010
ESC	(Escape)	027	0011011

Character		Integer Equivalent	Binary Equivalent
FS	(File Separator)	028	0011100
GS	(Group Separator)	029	0011101
RS	(Record Separator)	030	0011110
US	(Unit Separator)	031	0011111
SP	(Space)	032	0100000
!		033	0100001
"		034	0100010
#		035	0100011
$		036	0100100
%		037	0100101
&		038	0100110
'	(Closing Single Quote)	039	0100111
(		040	0101000
)		041	0101001
*		042	0101010
+		043	0101011
,	(Comma)	044	0101100
–	(Hyphen)	045	0101101
.	(Period)	046	0101110
/		047	0101111
0		048	0110000
1		049	0110001
2		050	0110010
3		051	0110011
4		052	0110100
5		053	0110101
6		054	0110110
7		055	0110111
8		056	0111000
9		057	0111001
:		058	0111010
;		059	0111011
<		060	0111100
=		061	0111101
>		062	0111110
?		063	0111111
@		064	1000000
A		065	1000001
B		066	1000010
C		067	1000011
D		068	1000100
E		069	1000101
F		070	1000110
G		071	1000111
H		072	1001000
I		073	1001001
J		074	1001010
K		075	1001011
L		076	1001100
M		077	1001101
N		078	1001110
O		079	1001111
P		080	1010000
Q		081	1010001
R		082	1010010

Character		Integer Equivalent	Binary Equivalent
S		083	1010011
T		084	1010100
U		085	1010101
V		086	1010110
W		087	1010111
X		088	1011000
Y		089	1011001
Z		090	1011010
[		091	1011011
\		092	1011100
]		093	1011101
^	(Circumflex Accent Mark)	094	1011110
_	(Underscore)	095	1011111
`	(Opening Single Quote)	096	1100000
a		097	1100001
b		098	1100010
c		099	1100011
d		100	1100100
e		101	1100101
f		102	1100110
g		103	1100111
h		104	1101000
i		105	1101001
j		106	1101010
k		107	1101011
l		108	1101100
m		109	1101101
n		110	1101110
o		111	1101111
p		112	1110000
q		113	1110001
r		114	1110010
s		115	1110011
t		116	1110100
u		117	1110101
v		118	1110110
w		119	1110111
x		120	1111000
y		121	1111001
z		122	1111010
{		123	1111011
			124	1111100
}		125	1111101
~		126	1111110
DEL	(Delete/Rubout)	127	1111111

Complete Solutions to Practice! Problems

SECTION 2.2, PAGE 27

1. valid
2. valid
3. invalid character (-), replacement `tax_rate`
4. valid
5. invalid character (^), replacement `sec_sqrd`
6. valid
7. valid
8. invalid, keyword, replacement `void_term`
9. invalid characters ((,)), replacement `fx`
10. invalid character (/), replacement `m_per_s`
11. valid
12. invalid character (.), replacement `w1_1`

SECTION 2.2, PAGE 28

1. 3.5004×10^1 3.5004e1   4 digits of precision
2. 4.2×10^{-4} 4.2e−4   1 digit of precision
3. -9.99×10^{-2} −9.99e−2   2 digits of precision
4. $1.00000028 \times 10^{-7}$ 1.00000028e−7   8 digits of precision
5. 0.0000103
6. −105000
7. −3552000
8. 0.000667

SECTION 2.2, PAGE 30

1. `const double LIGHT_SPEED=2.99792e8;`
2. `const double CHARGE_E=1.602177e-19;`
3. `const double G_MSS=9.8;`
4. `const double G_FTSS=32;`
5. `const double MOON_RADIUS=1.74e6;`

SECTION 2.3, PAGE 34

1. `4`   `3`   2. `4.5` 3. `3` 4. `3`

SECTION 2.3, PAGE 36

1. `tension = (2*m1*m2*g)/(m1 + m2);`
2. `P2 = P1 + rho*V2*V2*(A2*A2 - A1*A1)/(2*A1*A1);`
3. $\text{centripetal} = \dfrac{4\pi^2 r}{T^2}$
4. $\text{change} = GM_E m\left(\dfrac{1}{R_E} - \dfrac{1}{R_E + h}\right)$

SECTION 2.3, PAGE 40

1. x `3`   y `4`   z `8`

2. x `3`   y `4`   z `12`

3. x `6`   y `4`

4. x `2`   y `0`

SECTION 2.4, PAGE 43

1. `sum = 150`

   `average = 12.368`
2. `sum and average`
   `150    12.37`
3. `12.37 is the average;`
   `150 is the sum`
4. `12.37 is the average;    150 is the sum`

SECTION 2.5, PAGE 47

1.   -3   2.   -2   3.   0.125   4.   3.162278

SECTION 2.5, PAGE 48

1.   `length = k*sqrt(1 - (v/c)*(v/c));`
2.   `center = 38.1972*(r*r*r - s*s*s)*sin(a)/((r*r - s*s)*a);`
3.   range $= \dfrac{v_0^2}{g} \sin 2\theta$

4. $v = \sqrt{\dfrac{2gh}{1 + \dfrac{I}{mr^2}}}$

SECTION 3.2, PAGE 67

1.   true   2.   true   3.   true
4.   true   5.   true   6.   false

SECTION 3.3, PAGE 72

1.
```
if (time > 15)
    time++;
```
2.
```
if (sqrt(poly) < 0.5)
    cout << "poly = " << poly << endl;
```
3.
```
if (abs(volt_1-volt_2) > 10)
    cout << "volt_1: " << volt_1 << ",  volt_2: "
        << volt_2 << endl;
```
4.
```
if (log(x) >= 3)
{
    time = 0;
    count--;
}
```
5.
```
if (dist < 50 && time > 10)
    time += 2;
else
    time += 2.5;
```
6.
```
if (dist >= 100)
    time += 2;
else
    if (50<dist)
        time += 1;
    else
        time += 0.5;
```

SECTION 3.4, PAGE 78

1.	18	2.	18	3.	17
4.	9	5.	11	6.	infinite loop

SECTION 4.2, PAGE 111

1.   Actual Parameters   Formal Parameters

x	25	a	25
sqrt(x)	5	b	5
x-30	-5	c	-5

2.   2

SECTION 5.1, PAGE 122

1.

-5	4	3	0	0	0	0	0	0	0

2.

?	-5.5	5.5	5.5

3.

-.4	-.3	-.2	-.1	0	.1	.2	.3	.4

SECTION 5.1, PAGE 125

1.	3 8	2.	8
	15 21		30
	30 41		

SECTION 5.1, PAGE 127

1.	9.8	2.	9.8	3.	3.2	4.	1.5

SECTION 6.1, PAGE 137

1.	40	2.	60	3.	71	4.	103
5.	O	6.	$	7.	u	8.	^

Index

Precedence	Operation	Associativity	Page
1	( ) [ ]	innermost first	xx
2	++ -- + - ! cast	right to left (unary)	xx
3	* / %	left to right	xx
4	+ -	left to right	xx
5	< <= > >=	left to right	xx
6	== !=	left to right	xx
7	&&	left to right	xx
8	||	left to right	xx
9	= += -= *= /= %=	right to left	xx

Elementary Math Functions

ceil(x)	exp(x)	fabs(x)	floor(x)
log(x)	log10(x)	pow(x,y)	sqrt(x)

Trigonometric Functions

acos(x)	asin(x)	atan(x)	atan2(y,x)
cos(x)	sin(x)	tan(x)	

Character Functions

isalnum(c)	isalpha(c)	iscntrl(c)	isdigit(c)
isgraph(c)	islower(c)	isprint(c)	ispunct(c)
isspace(c)	isupper(c)	isxdigit(c)	tolower(c)
toupper(c)			

Input Operator: >>
Output Operator: <<
Manipulators:
```
setw(size);
setprecision(digit);
setfill(char);
```

Preprocessor directives

```
#include <iostream.h>
#define FILENAME "sensor1.dat"
```

Declarations and Definitions

```
const double PI=3.141593;
int year_1, year_2, count=0, n[]={2,4,6};
double x[25];
char c = '*';
double sinc(double x);
```

Assignment statement

```
area = 0.5*base*(height_1 + height_2);
```

I/O statements

```
cout << "The area is " << area << " square feet" << endl;
cin >> year;
sensor1 >> time >> motion;
balloon << time << altitude << velocity;
cin.get(c);
cout.put(c);
```

Program exit statements

```
return EXIT_SUCCESS;
return count;
return;
```

If statements

```
if (d <= 30)
    velocity = 4.25 + 0.00175*d*d;
else
    velocity = 0.65 + 0.12*d - 0.0025*d*d;
```

While loop

```
while (degrees <= 360)
{
    cout << degrees << "   " << degrees*PI/180 << endl;
    degrees += 10;
}
```

Do/while loop

```
do
{
    cout << degrees << "   " << degrees*PI/180 << endl;
    degrees += 10;
} while (degrees <= 360);
```

For loop

```
for (int degrees=0; degrees<=360; degrees+=10)
    cout << degrees << "   " << degrees*PI/180 << endl;
```

File open/close functions

```
fstream sensor1;
sensor1.open("sensor1.dat", ios::in);
sensor1.close();
```